Following this is a comparison of the Christian prescription for the recovery of community through responsible love and the secular prescription offered by the social analyst. And in the closing chapters, Dr. Beach applies both theories to politics, race, and the "multiversity" with its student upheavals.

Added advantage: a vocabulary of sharp, vivid, image-conjuring words and phrases that the reader can use to make discussion more meaningful.

THE AUTHOR

WALDO BEACH is Professor of Christian Ethics and Director of Graduate Studies in Religion at Duke University. An alumnus of Wesleyan and Yale Universities, he has taught religion at Antioch College, Pacific School of Religion, and Union Theological Seminary in New York. He has lectured at Northwestern University, Austin Presbyterian Theological Seminary, Texas Christian University, and Union Theological Seminary in Richmond.

Christian Community
and American Society

Christian Community and American Society

by
Waldo Beach

The Westminster Press · Philadelphia

1. Sociology, Christian
2. United States - Social Conditions -- 1945-

Standard Book No. 664–20854–1
Library of Congress Catalog Card No. 69–14196

PUBLISHED BY THE WESTMINSTER PRESS®
PHILADELPHIA, PENNSYLVANIA

PRINTED IN THE UNITED STATES OF AMERICA

To R.W.B., M.A.B., and E.A.B., in the hope that their America may understand the terms of Christian community

Preface

This volume is a study of American society today as illumined and judged by the ethical norms of Christian community. As such it moves in thought between two disciplines: Christian ethics on the one side, as a normative science setting the terms of the good life as understood in the Hebrew-Christian tradition, and sociology on the other, as a descriptive science. When the Christian ethicist and secular social scientist engage in sustained dialogue, they may learn much from each other. The book is ventured in the confidence that the insights of the Christian faith are pertinent to the condition of the American, experiencing as he does the "loss of community" in his mechanized, urbanized, crowd existence. From the self-scrutiny of American society by the sociologist, the Christian may learn much of himself and of what explains the failure of his conventional institutional Christianity to speak to his real corporate needs.

In its present form, the volume represents the reworking of materials taught for a span of several years in graduate seminars in the Duke University Graduate School of Arts and Sciences. Some of these chapters are extensions and revisions of the Shaffer Lectures at Northwestern University, and the Oreon E. Scott Lectures at Texas Christian University. The author would like to record here his appreciation to these two universities for the honor of giving these lectures, and for many courtesies of hospitality during his stay on their campuses. The final chapter, "Christian Community and the American University," first appeared in the *Emory University Quarterly* (Vol. XXIII, No. 2, Summer, 1967, pp. 110 ff.) and in edited form is included here with the gracious permission of the editor, Dr. Jack Boozer.

Acknowledgment is further due to the American Association of Theological Schools for fellowship subvention for sabbatical study and research.

A word of special thanks goes to these individuals for various forms of wise editorial and indefatigable clerical help: Dana Wilbanks, Richard Beauchamp, Paul Johnson, Mrs. Joyce Farris, Mrs. Nancy Fulcher, and Mrs. Marie Davis.

W. B.

Durham, North Carolina

Contents

I

The Theological Ground of Community

On first glance, the task to which this volume sets itself might seem a simple exercise: to delineate the meaning of the term "community." Yet little probing is needed to show that the word conveys complex and subtle meanings, with shades varying according to the variety of contexts in which it is used. A city planner and a mystic would have some trouble conversing on the subject. For a theologian, a historian, a political scientist, a sociologist, a philosopher, "community" might mean totally different things. At best, the areas of shared meaning would be small. In common usage, the disparities in meaning of the word are even greater. It would certainly be a considerable distance between the concept of community found in Augustine's *City of God* and the ideal implicit in the advertisement on the back cover of *Life,* celebrating a brand of beer whose consumption is conducive to the *Gemütlichkeit* of family jollity, the tribal pleasures of fellowship and affluence. The community that prevails in the choir of angels in harmony around the heavenly throne would bear little resemblance to the beatific vision on the ruddy faces of those enjoying fellowship in Budweiser.

Toward Dialogue Between Theology and Social Science

Our special interest in this volume is to explore and compare the meaning of community as it is understood on the one hand in the Christian faith and on the other hand in contemporary sociological analyses of American society. This entails an attempt to resume or start a conversation between theologian and sociologist, talk that for a long time, at least in America, has been at best strained and artificial, and for the most part nonexistent. In most universities today the theologian and sociologist are not on good speaking terms. Yet it is the bold—perhaps foolhardy—thesis of the pages that follow that when they are speaking substantively about what constitutes good community, there are surprising similarities in what they say, at least significant areas of agreement in the normative meaning of words, even within disagreement about the truth-claims of each side.

In arranging a meaningful conversation between Christian theologian and social scientist, on any matters of substance, many matters of methodology need to be examined and misunderstandings on both sides cleared away. To start with, talk would be hampered by common stereotypes fixed in the minds of both parties. To the sociologist, it is assumed that the theologian operates on faith, which means the explication of dogma revealed from on high, through mystic flash of insight or ecclesiastical or Biblical decree. On matters of ethics, the theologian is expected to preach or moralize. To the theologian, on the other side, the sociologist is assumed to operate by scientific reason, as a cold empiricist, describing only facts of social behavior, exempted from any value preferences or moral judgments. He is a nose counter, a statistician. How can a preacher talk with a computer? Little headway can be made into significant exchange until these stereotypes are corrected, and other ground rules are acknowledged, more true to the subtle admixture of faith and reason and of the normative and descriptive that obtains in the disciplines of both theology and sociology.

The Problem of Knowledge in Sociology and Theology

To explicate the varieties and theories of knowledge in Christian theology and in current sociology would take us into intricacies far beyond the intention of this study[1] or the competence of this student, but certain working assumptions of method will need to be set forth. As any serious conversation between theologian and social scientist develops, when both are dismantled from their pontifical robes, it becomes evident that the exchange is not between dogmatism and empiricism, or between blind faith and skeptical reason. There are appeals to experience in every sophisticated theology and faithful elements in every social scientist, a priori assumptions that cannot be authenticated by sheer accumulation of facts. True, the reasoning of a theologian may be done from out of a circle of primal faith in the reality of God. But he is obliged to responsible reflection on the implications of his faith for those aspects of human experience which confirm or correct his position. The sociologist who rules out such a faith standpoint as illegitimate—following LaPlace's classic dismissal of the question why he did not believe in God, "Sir, I have no need of that hypothesis"—may be as rigid and dogmatic in his epistemology as any of the church fathers were supposed to be. The rejoinder to his earnest protest that no man has seen God at any time might be to say that no man has seen a value system at any time, or *anomie* or alienation or, for that matter, society. In dialogue with the theologian, a sociologist may defend a dogma of radical empiricism such as affirmed by Lord Kelsen: "Only that is knowledge which can be weighed and measured." But in such dialogue it is faith against faith, not faith against fact.

By and large the dominant trend in current sociological theory is away from the image of sociology as organized statistics and toward the use of root concepts which are qualitative, psychological, even "poetic."[2] This does not imply that sociologists are being converted in droves to the Christian faith. But it does mean that, once the stereotypes are transcended, intelligible and fruitful dialogue becomes possible, on the assumption of a shared use of faith and reason, rationalism and empiricism, a priori assumptions and a posteriori empirical testing, in both enterprises of theology and sociology in their attempts to discern the contours and lineaments of reality. Just as there is no such thing as presuppositionless thinking in sociology, so there is no exemption from empirical testing in theology, though the criteria of verification in theology may be differently conceived from what empiricism usually would admit.

From which side should the conversation begin? We might well listen first to the sociologist, as he defines community, to detect the hidden norms and criteria that underlie his descriptions.[3] It will serve our purpose better, however, to listen first to Christian theology. Granted that the Hebrew-Christian faith is but one of the world's major religions, and that all have great wisdom about the nature of man and community, we are justified in taking Christianity as the point of departure, since it has been the dominant faith in the West and has deeply informed its cultural institutions.

How is the word "community" understood in the Christian tradition? The first answer one hears is a babble of voices. There are many Christian positions. To take one for normative would seem arbitrary indeed. We need to pay close attention to the heritage of Roman Catholic scholasticism and to the many voices of Protestant persuasion.[4] The divergence in thought-forms cannot be squeezed into a simple unanimity. The categories of Roman Catholic (and to a considerable degree Anglican) thinking are scholastic in tone: rationalistic, Aristotelian, abstract, essential, ontological, Greek, visual in imagery. The categories of Protestant thought, on the other hand, are more graphic, Biblical, dramatic, existential, concrete, personalistic, Hebraic, audial in imagery.

Yet withal, by contrast with the world view of a naturalistic positivism (in general still the established world view of social science) the differences among Christian views prove to be more of emphasis than of core substance. There is a strong consensus in the ecumenical Christian community about the basic meaning of the terms that concern us in this study.[5] A Protestant observer at the Vatican Council would find himself much more intellectually at home than at a meeting of the American Sociological Society. The great axioms of Christian faith, the primacy of the Transcendent, the dependence of the temporal upon the Eternal, the creatureliness of man as made in the image of God, the eschatological dimension of man's worldly destiny, the sacred setting of the secular, God's rule over man in history—whatever the debate about the shades of meaning of these terms—these axioms inform all Christian discussion of the meaning of community. So we may fairly proceed to speak of *the* Christian position, representing this strong consensus, acknowledging as we go the persisting varieties.

Community as Quality of Relations

Both in its historical and contemporary forms, the word "community" is understood in Christian thought in a *relational* sense. Put simply, it has to do with the quality of relations among persons. As a formal definition, "community" of whatever sort is present—quite apart from whether it be good or bad, authentic or inauthentic—in the interaction of persons with each other and within the total context of their life together. It has to do not with the substance, or essence, of the interacting parts, but with the quality or style of the traffic of their relationship. It appears at the point of the "between," or the "inter," between man and man, or between man and God, or man and nature.

This relational meaning of the word is characteristic of many key terms in Christian ethical theory. The prepositions give the clue to the meaning. In Christian discourse, "love" by itself is an empty abstraction: the distinctive quality of love is derived from its relation to its object. "Faith" is a meaningless term unless the "in" is added. To mean anything, "freedom" requires the implied "from" and the "for" that follow. So with the word "community." It is not the description and collection of the component parts that define it, but the pattern of relationship among the members.

A second feature in the basic concept of community is that the quality of relations is defined *internally,* by reference to the inner purposes or wills of its relating members. A "community" is different from a "society," or "association" (as the German *Gemeinschaft* is different from *Gesellschaft*),[6] in that it is constituted by some kind of internal relation of interdependence, a shared and mutual interest and participation in a common object,[7] whereas the word "society," or "association," connotes a collectivity of persons whose relation is only external and physical.

A third formal element in the Christian concept of community is that it has to do with the total reach and scope of human relations. Its dimensions are not merely societal and interpersonal but extend to the relations of man to the world of nature, and to whatever is taken as ultimate beyond nature. There is an inevitably cosmic relation hidden or explicit in every serious conception of community: how men relate to each other and to nature is a function of how they feel as related to whatever is taken as the final reality, or "object of ultimate concern," to use Paul Tillich's phrase. This object may be negative, an abyss, a cosmic blank, as for nihilistic existentialism. Or it may be some universalized projection of man onto the cosmic blank, where the ultimate is taken as society, or mankind, or the state. Or, with classic monotheistic religions, the ultimate object may be a transcendent One, the creative and ruling force, the source and ground of all things, God. As explicated in the chapters to follow, community, as understood in the Christian tradition, is grounded in and makes its final sense out of its faith in God and the manner of his rule. The fact that one or another social scientist or analyst of culture cannot in conscience share this premise of faith need not mean, however, that the conversation must break off at the start. Both parties at least may acknowledge that *some* sort of cosmic referent, theistic or atheistic, informs and colors their reflection on the mystery of human existence in the world.

In turning now to review the primer points of Christian theology that pertain to the norm of community, we make use first of Biblical categories. We might as readily use scholastic categories to put more abstractly the reality caught in graphic and poetic Biblical terms. The graphic and poetic imagery of the Biblical myths, the giant anthropomorphisms used in Genesis to describe God's action, and the earthy Hebraic language of blood and heart used to describe human response, need not tax credulity if they are taken in the sense intended: as poetic, dramatic imagery to catch a quality of reality that escapes the quantitative or abstract language of the laboratory scientist or philosopher. Withal, the perils as well as the aptness of dramatic metaphor need to be remembered.

Community as Covenant of God and Man

In the Bible, from first to last, community is understood as a covenant relationship between God and man.[8] God the sovereign creator is subject. In a sequence of concrete historical events, he calls into existence the original order of community in Eden, then elects a people of his choice in the covenant of law with Israel, then sets the terms of a new covenant in Christ and a new community, the church, which lives in the promise of a final consummation and triumph of the divine purpose. All these constitute a historic drama of creation, fall, judgment, redemption, and consummation, a drama in which man plays his role as responding subject. The modes of his response to the actions of God determine the quality of his relations in community to his fellows. The primal reference is the vertical relation of man to the Lord of the covenant, in obedience to or defection from God's rule.

Another root metaphor or master image of Biblical theology is that of the "Kingdom of God." This monarchical metaphor, taken from the political power structure of the tiny Jewish kingdoms of ancient Palestine, conveys the conviction that the terms of men's relations to each other and to nature are set according to an absolute and inexorable divine rule. God is King of the universe, the Lord of history. Even in the disorder that follows from man's defection from the covenant, his rule is evident. Though the term "Kingdom of God" has undergone many changes of meaning in the history of Christian thought,[9] its Biblical root meaning can be taken as normative: community as the quality of relationships of men as they stand under the kingship of God.

Community in the Ontological Order

As already noted, Roman Catholic thought describes the theological ground of community in more rational, analytic, and abstract terms. Behind the modern papal encyclicals, the documents of the Vatican Council, or the reflections of contemporary

Roman Catholic social philosophers, such as Jacques Maritain, Gabriel Marcel, and Christopher Dawson, is the ancient scholastic wisdom, incorporating Aristotelian philosophy, Roman jurisprudence, and Augustinian theology into the medieval synthesis. In its modern form Catholicism weaves many strands of nineteenth-century secular thought into its dense fabric. For Catholic social philosophy, human community is understood as derived from an ontological structure given in the very nature of things, a structure derived from the Being of God. The structure of created being is hierarchical, ordered in a scale or ladder in which the order of being is also the order of value. God, at the top of the scale, is the source and culmination of total being and total worth in himself. Below God, the angelic, the human, the animal, the inanimate, descend in that order down to nothing, or nonbeing.[10] The significance of this concept for our problem of the nature of community lies in the belief that the relations that constitute authentic community depend on right position in the scale of being. Disorder is derangement or the displacement of the parts from their divinely intended good order. This grand premise is still, albeit in an attenuated sense, axiomatic for modern secular thought and discourse. When certain kinds of human behavior are called degrading or bestial, something akin to the scale of being and of value is implied. Human beings should act befitting their place on the scale.

The other major theme informing all Roman Catholic thinking about community is that of natural law. According to Thomas Aquinas—and all subsequent Catholic thought faithful to him—the constitution of all things lies in the structures of law: (1) eternal law in the mind of God, (2) natural law as the perception of the principles of eternal law by rational creatures, (3) human or positive laws, valid insofar as in accord with natural law, and (4) divine law, the special modes of law given by revelation in Scripture.[11] The natural law tradition affirms an ontological foundation for the superstructure of true human community. The quality of right or authentic relationships among men does not depend on the variety of cultural circumstances or the relative artifices of human convenience but upon the nature of man as created in the image of God, and endowed with a rational and immortal soul.

Man as Creature

Augustine recounts somewhere his encounter in imagination with one of God's angels, who asks him what he would like above all else to know. His reply is: the nature of God and the nature of man. "Anything else?" asks the angel. "Nothing else," replies Augustine. Christian anthropology in its conception of the nature of man is as crucial a premise in understanding Christian community as is the Christian conception of the nature of God. Certain Biblical motifs are axiomatic for ecumenical thought about man, Protestant[12] or Catholic.

The first is that man's unique identity is derived from a divine source. Whether expressed in the mythology of Genesis, in the poetry of The Psalms, in the aphorisms of Jesus, or in the more sophisticated philosophic categories of Paul, the common assumption about man is that he is creature, created in the image of God, whose very being is theonomous and whose dignity is one derived from a divine source.

The Biblical doctrine of man is always concrete and personal. It asks: Who is man? rather than: What is humanity? The answer is given in relational terms. "What is man that thou art mindful of him?"—the psalmist's rhetorical question is put in terms of his relation to God. As creature, a man finds his identity, his selfhood, in his encounter with the divine Other.

The Greek thinking about human nature behind scholasticism casts the problem in terms of whether man is "body" or "mind," or how both. The Hebraic way of thinking about man behind Protestantism is voluntaristic, centering on the will of man, beneath body and mind, as the crucial factor. A man is as he loves. His inner identity is to be defined in terms of that which he prizes above all in his universe.[13] He becomes like that toward which he orients his existence. In Biblical terms, "where your treasure is, there will your heart be also." This simply puts graphically his relational nature. To say that he is created in the image of

God is to say that his unique selfhood is defined by that which is "above" him in the scale of creation rather than by the relation to what is "below." Here, as we shall see later, is a crucial dividing line between Christian anthropology and the dominant secular anthropologies whose primary reference is to "downward" comparisons, conceiving of man in the image of the animal.

Man in Community

A second feature of Biblical anthropology is its corporate character. Man is in created essence a societal self, or "solidaristic," as Roman Catholic terminology puts it. "It is not good that the man should be alone," speaks the creator God of Genesis. In contrast to the Greek tradition, which can conceive of man as a self-contained individual, the bearer of reason, the Hebraic-Christian way of conceiving man never abstracts his selfhood from the living historical context of a people. In the Old Testament, there is no substantive disjunction between the "I" and the "we," between the self and the house of Israel. And in the New Testament, though there are occasional notes of individualism, the Christian member of the new community understands his identity by organic relation to the body of Christ.

This axiom of the "corporate personality" of man—to anticipate a bit the lines of the argument to follow—is of crucial importance. For as we shall see, it stands in contrast to two polar-opposite anthropologies of modern Western thought: radical individualism and radical collectivism. In the individualism assumed in much eighteenth- and nineteenth-century ethics, politics, and economics, the "ultimate" self is a self-contained identity, who has, to be sure, social relations of every kind, but for whose essence these associations are accidental. In the Biblical world view, on the other hand, the very "being" of a man lies "in between" the "I" and the plural others, human and transcendent, with whom he is in dialogue.[14]

On the other hand, the corporate image of man is not the collectivistic view underlying modern totalitarianism. "Mass man" of East or West has lost his uniqueness, his separate identity in his passionate or resigned loyalty to a finite God of a political or economic sort. Lacking any transcendent point of detachment from the crowd, his identity is reduced to a mechanical likeness to all the others in the sand heap. In the Biblical view, by contrast, there is individuality—not individualism—in that man is called by One beyond the crowd, by a Voice addressing him in his uniqueness, to whom he responds in obedience. Herein is the significance of the Biblical preoccupation with names and naming. "I have called you by name," says the Lord. In the physical, animal, and human worlds, the richness of diverse kinds is preserved in the God-given names of all creatures. The divine "Thou" calls a man into being with a name of his own and emancipates him from the tyranny of the collective.

Within this corporate or solidaristic view of man-in-community, there are many familiar features of anthropology developed by Roman and Reformed versions of the Christian faith. Scholastic theology has explored in detail the analytic view of the self, in terms of body, will, intellect, and conscience, celebrating the dignity of man as crown of creation and by these attributes distinguished from the animal.[15] Protestant theology has cast the same matter in more Biblical and existential terms: man is seen in action, as a loving or hating creature, choosing, seeking, struggling with self, with neighbor, with God. It is an assumption shared by all Christian thinkers, even extreme Calvinists, that in some sense man is distinct from nature in having a freedom of will, though freedom is conceived always in the context of a divine rule. It is a crucial, dreadful freedom; the consequences of his choice ring with the overtones of eternity.

This is all an exalted view of human nature. When political rhetoric speaks of "the sacredness of self" or "the dignity of man" it echoes authentically Biblical anthropology. But the sacredness or dignity is theonomously derived; man has a dignity derived from a divine source, a sacredness first in the sight of God, and thence in the sight of men.

Community in the Order of Creation

We may recast something of what has already been said in terms of the quality of community as constituted by the relations of man in the three conditions archetypal in Biblical and classical Protestant theology: (1) the original order of life in creation, (2) the fallen order of man's life under the conditions of sin, and (3) the order of grace and redemption. If these be construed not as chronological epochs or periods along a time line, but as descriptions of qualities of existence encountered simultaneously, in varying proportions at any moment of history, they provide theological insight of a distinctive sort in man's self-understanding and his quest for community.

The Genesis story is the archetypal myth of community in the order of creation. It has its parallels, of course, in many of the world's religions. It is axiomatic for much of Western literature, philosophy, and art—all at least that views the present as in some sense a loss of or defection from some original condition of primal purity and perfection. In creation, it is affirmed, man stands in a certain "given" order of right relationship. It is at once the order of being and the order of value, as caught in Augustine's famous dictum: "Whatever is, is good," in its created essence.

Community in creation means a right order of priority on the scale of creation. Where Adam is set in the garden, according to the poetry of Genesis, with "all things under his feet," to till and keep the garden for his use and delight, he stands in right relation to nature. When the papal encyclicals speak of the dignity of man as inhering in his possession of property, as a "natural right" of having footing in soil of his own—this same norm is echoed.[16] But Adam is not Lord of creation; he is subservient to the Creator. Before the Fall his "upward" relation is one of innocent obedience to God, in reverence, and in innocent love to neighbor. Presumably, the sexual relations of Adam and Eve were devoid of lust. The domestic peace in the community of the garden was the concord of innocence. Adam's freedom was the freedom of glad obedience to the Creator's will and the terms of the original covenant, unmarred by doubt or protest. Presumably, too, in his free obedience to God, Adam experienced his pure identity.

The Fall of Man

This "original" community—"original" now to be read in an ontological, not chronological, sense—is broken by man's prideful rebellion in the Fall. In the misuse of his created freedom, according to classical Christian theology, man defies the terms of the covenant community, claims to be "as God," and alters the terms of community relations. The consequence of his defiance is an estrangement or alienation in every dimension of his existence. He is separated from God as the source of his life, who now ominously stands over against him, as threat, stranger, enemy. He is alienated from neighbor, in strife and competition. The other man is rival to be fought or object to be used, not subject to be loved. Fear and lust now taint all neighbor relations, whether intimate or distant. Man "falls" from the identity of innocence. He experiences alienation from self, ambiguity of moral doubt, the internal division of body, mind, and will, a dread in the dizziness of freedom, the sense of guilt and failure. Finally, man is alienated from nature, which is turned from bountiful garden to recalcitrant and accursed foe, that now must be worked with the sweat of his brow.

In this pervasive disorganization of life in the Fall, the original "power structure" of the created order, where man's power *over* nature but *under* God is rightly used, is now deranged. The "given" powers of creation are now turned from theocentric to egocentric or partisan ends. Man's powers of intelligence are turned to self-justification in self-defensive thinking and deceit. Man's physical power is turned to violence against his neighbor. Man's creative and aesthetic powers are turned to self-aggrandizement. The distinctive powers of ethnic differences are turned to partisan ends (white superiority or Black Power). Human existence becomes the war of every man against every man.

In the tradition of the Christian faith, this "broken community" yet remains under the sovereignty of God. The structure of relations in the Fall is still a perversion or derangement of that which remains, behind the disorder, fundamentally ordered and good, in much the same way as medical science interprets sickness as a dysfunctioning within the normal functioning order of health. Under God's rule, there are "built-in" limits and restraints to man's defiance of the created order, the process of God's judgment, present in the structures of punishment for man's sin. Under the divine sovereignty, there is then a secondary community, a covenant of law, or call it "negative community," which keeps a kind of order or "peace" within the conditions and consequences of sin. The concept of negative community implicit in Paul, explicit in Augustine, Luther, Calvin, and many contemporary theologians, provides a most intriguing clue to the Christian analysis of contemporary culture.

Community Restored

The third of order of community is that of grace, under the aspect of God the Redeemer. For that which makes the Christian faith a gospel of redemption is its claim that the one God who as Creator brings into being the order of all things, and who as governor limits and restrains man in his misuse of creation, is also the one who redeems and restores all things, in the forgiveness of grace.

The manner of the operation of divine grace in history is variously described and contended in the history of Christian thought. How to relate divine initiative and human response, "works" and "faith," how "common" grace in nature and history is related to "special" grace in Jesus Christ, where grace can be expected to appear in culture, in the sacred or in the secular, inside or outside the institutional church: these constitute the questions for continuing unresolved debate among Christians. But there is a deep consensus underneath the diversity: the faith that beyond whatever restorative aspects of grace that appear universally in nature, there is given to man in the incarnation—in the total event of Christ, his life, person, teaching, and death—a special grace. Christ sets the terms of a new covenant, and a new community. The moral terms of the new covenant are embodied in the total style and bearing of the earthly life of Christ, and his death on the cross: *agape* love. God's love incarnate in Christ becomes the "means of grace" for those in the new community who carry his name, and whose response is a comparable love toward neighbor, forgiving one another as they have been forgiven.

The consequences of the redeeming activity of God in Christ are the restoration of right order out of disorder, the reconciliation of man with man and of man with nature. For man, as recipient of grace, the experience inwardly is one of guilt lifted, confidence granted, the moral nerve of action restored. God becomes no longer enemy, but friend. Outwardly, and along the horizontal plane, the peace of concord is restored, but it is the peace of forgiveness, not the original peace of childhood innocence; it is the wise and sober peace of maturity. In the community of grace, the direction of love is converted from egocentricity into a will to seek the common and universal good. The bearing of the ethical consequence of response to grace will be explicated in the next chapter.

The Locus of God's Kingdom Within Space and Time

In this cursory review of those salient points of Christian theology which bear on the problem of community, it remains, finally, to consider *where* community is to be located in space and time.

On this as on other matters Biblical mythology is consistently historical and concrete. The great events and crises of men's life in community are cast as real and dramatic events that take place along a real time line and in flesh-and-blood persons. From the original creation of Adam and Eve in Eden, through the events of the Fall, the exodus, the giving of the law on Sinai, the messianic promises, the incarnation, the establishment of the new community of the church, through to the promised consummation—these are historical events. For the Hebraic mind, and the mind of the early church, they are to be taken on the same plane of historicity, univocally, as real happenings, transpired or expected. The movement of man's life in history is along a line of time: the good order of creation in Eden is broken by the Fall, the condition of exile and alienation for the people of Israel is the epoch of judgment, and the curse of life under the law, brightened only by hints and prophecies of a Messiah to come. Then in Christ the new order begins, and after Christ the new community of grace and redemption appears and spreads. The new order is mixed with and contends with the old until the final eschatological close of the drama, in the great consummation of God's victory expected.[17]

For the twentieth-century mind—and especially for the social scientist who is to be party to our dialogue—this kind of philosophy of history constitutes a stumbling block and foolishness. In what sense are these myths to be understood by the contemporary child of Copernicus and the scientific revolution? Can he take them "seriously, but not literally," as in Reinhold Niebuhr's bold but too-simple prescription? The demythologizing controversy in current Biblical theology (as with the older debate about "realized eschatology") marks the realization of the twentieth-century student that he simply cannot transplant intact a literal Biblical eschatology from the first century into the present, as providing the categories for the explanation of historical chronology, any more than he can transplant the pre-Copernican cosmology of the Bible, with its terracentric, three-storied universe, as a picture of things adequate to the space age.

Very serious reinterpretations of these Biblical categories are needed before intelligible dialogue between theologian and the historian or social scientist can take place. The point of view here adopted is that the classic myths of the Bible are in one sense to be taken in a transtemporal yet intrahistorical way. They are true myths in much the same sense as are certain classic myths of social philosophy, e.g., the institution of private property in the *gens* state for Marx, or the institution of government by social contract for Locke. The Biblical myths, creation, Fall, judgment, redemption, are to be taken not as temporal epochs, one closing off before the other begins, but as simultaneous dynamic processes occurring within history, all detectable to the eyes of faith within any one epoch. God *is* creating an order of harmony and interdependence; he *is* overruling that order through structures of rewards and punishments appearing within all the human disruptions of that order; and he *is* ever restoring through his grace the pattern of concord. Such an interpretation of God's action preserves the historicity of the Biblical interpretation but in a fashion freed from the crudities of Biblical literalism. By this reading of things, the eschatological dimension of the Christian view is kept. The Kingdom of God is not located at the end of a time line, as in versions of Christian Utopias, but breaks in on the present, is "realized" now. As the Kingdom impinges on the present, it gives to decision an urgency lacking in the dynamics of Utopian reflection. "Every moment in time is equidistant from eternity." This aphorism would be a Greek way of casting the Hebraic-Christian affirmation: "The Kingdom of God is at hand."[18]

The same clue may be fruitful in dealing with the problem of the locus of Christian community in space. What kind of Christian cartography might make sense to modern man, spinning in centerless and unbounded space and dizzy from cultural relativism? By the same token as for their use in time, the great myths and metaphors might illumine the human condition when universalized, i.e., when read in a transspatial sense. The validity of the Biblical myths does not hang on whether a terracentric or a heliocentric picture is the more accurate. For the criterion of the credibility of Biblical myths cannot be their empirical accuracy as accounts of fact, but their relevance to the predicaments of man's historical condition.

One can say then that man's alienation prevails as much "west of Eden" as "east of Eden." It is no closer to one civilization than to another. It is equidistant from all man's cultural or "natural" institutions, family, state, economy, the church. The claim is that there is nothing inherent in the relations of the structure of the nuclear family, per se, that assures its embodiment of community more than the larger circles of the state or the economy. Order-alienation-reconciliation, peace and strife, love and hate, these perennial dynamic polarities permeate all social institutions among the children of man.

In sum, if one may put the matter more dramatically, when one asks about the locus of Christian community, its where and when, the answers are as elusive as the questions are earnestly put by all commuters in time and space. Christian community, like the Kingdom of God, is a transtemporal, transspatial reality, equidistant, like eternity, from every moment in time or every spot in space. It appears here or there, intermittently, ambiguously, in the midways of man's life, as close as God's grace and as far as man's sin. It is daily granted to men with the wheeling stars and the morning sun, daily despoiled in man's pride and power, and daily restored by grace as the ground of his hope and the promise of his search.

NOTES

1. The epistemological debate continues among theologians and social scientists with not even a consensus in prospect in either discipline. Among theologians, the lines have shifted considerably since the days of D. C. MacIntosh, *The Problem of Religious Knowledge* (Harper & Brothers, 1940). See Erich Frank, *Philosophical Understanding and Religious Truth* (Oxford University Press, Inc., 1945); John Hick, *Faith and Knowledge: A Modern Introduction to the Problem of Religious Knowledge* (Cornell University Press, 1957); Martin D'Arcy, *The Nature of Belief* (London: Sheed & Ward, Ltd., 1931); William Blackstone, *The Problem of Religious Knowledge* (Prentice-Hall, Inc., 1963). In current sociology, a few of the best guides to the issues are: Felix Kaufman, *Methodology of the Social Sciences* (Oxford University Press, Inc., 1944); Maurice Natanson (ed.), *Philosophy of the Social Sciences* (Random House, Inc., 1963); and Max Weber, *The Methodology of the Social Sciences,* tr. and ed. by Edward A. Shils and Henry Finch (The Free Press of Glencoe, Inc., 1949). Peter Berger's *Invitation to Sociology* (Doubleday & Company, Inc., 1963) is a sprightly introduction to the problem. Michael Polanyi's *Personal Knowledge* (The University of Chicago Press, 1958) has proved a major breakthrough.

2. See, for example, Maurice R. Stein and Arthur J. Vidich (eds.), *Sociology on Trial* (Prentice-Hall, Inc., 1963), which explicates the recovery of the classical philosophic assumptions of the "fathers" of modern sociology, such as Weber, Simmel, Durkheim, Mannheim, Myrdal, C. Wright Mills, Merton, Parsons, Riesman, and many others, who espouse normative and qualitative concepts transcending superficial empiricism. Chapter IV below explores these matters in more detail.

3. Such an approach is to be found in Gibson Winter, *Elements for a Social Ethic: Scientific and Ethical Perspectives on Social Process* (The Macmillan Company, 1966). A comparable attempt to strike up conversation between sociology and philosophy is Edward Tiryakian, *Sociologism and Existentialism* (Prentice-Hall, Inc., 1962).

4. Not to speak of the Eastern Orthodox tradition increasingly heard in Western ecumenical circles, or the Jewish existential mysticism of Martin Buber.

5. See, for example, the four volumes preparatory to the World Council of Churches Geneva Conference in 1966. While the disagreement in these volumes (and at the Conference) proved intense on issues of policy, the assumptions about the norms of the "responsible society" reflected a "substantial consensus." See John C. Bennett (ed.), *Christian Social Ethics in a Changing World* (Association Press, 1966), p. 135. This volume, together with the other three preparatory study volumes, and the official report of the Conference, *Christians in the Technical and Social Revolutions of Our Time,* World Conference on Church and Society (Geneva: World Council of Churches, 1967), are heavily used in this study.

6. See Ferdinand Tönnies, *Community and Society,* tr. by Charles P. Loomis (Michigan State University Press, 1957).

7. Augustine's classic definition of a *civitas,* or city, as formed by a mutual agreement on the common object of love (*The City of God,* XIX. xiii–xiv) has been normative for social philosophy in the West, Christian and non-Christian. The contemporary World Council volume *Man in Community,* ed. by Egbert de Vries (Association Press, 1966), plays many variations on the Augustinian theme.

8. The discussion here telescopes many complex issues of Biblical theology. It relies primarily on such materials as G. Ernest Wright, *The Biblical Doctrine of Man in Society* (London: SCM Press, Ltd., 1960); H. Wheeler Robinson, *Religious Ideas of the Old Testament* (Charles Scribner's Sons, 1921); E. C. Rust, *Nature and Man in Biblical Thought* (London: Lutterworth Press, 1953); Walter Eichrodt, *Man in the Old Testament,* tr. by K. and R. Gregor Smith (London: Henry Regnery Company, 1951).

9. See H. Richard Niebuhr, *The Kingdom of God in America* (Willett, Clark, & Company, 1937).

10. The principle of the hierarchy of being is of course not exclusive to Roman Catholicism but is a major axiom of Western Christian thought in general. For its place in the history of ideas, see Arthur O. Lovejoy, *The Great Chain of Being* (Harvard University Press, 1936). Leslie Dewart's *The Future of Belief* (Herder & Herder, Inc., 1966) is one of several Roman Catholic books currently challenging the neat ontological order of the scholastic scheme.

11. Thomas Aquinas, *Summa Theologica,* II, section on the Laws (qq. 90–108).

12. To speak of Protestant anthropology is, of course, a gross foreshortening of major varieties. Yet there remains a surprising degree of consensus within such different classical statements of Christian anthropology as Reinhold Niebuhr's *Nature and Destiny of Man* (Charles Scribner's Sons, 1941–1943); Emil Brunner's *Man in Revolt,* tr. by Olive Wyon (Charles Scribner's Sons, 1939); H. Richard Niebuhr's *The Responsible Self* (Harper & Row, Publishers, Inc., 1963); and the various essays in the ecumenical symposium *Man in Community,* ed. by de Vries.

13. Roman Catholic anthropology, of course, is a complex synthesis of Greek rationalism with Hebraic voluntarism. The dominant emphasis in classical Roman thought is on the reason as guiding the will, but both will *and* reason are central. In many contemporary Catholic writers, such as Bernard Häring, the will assumes priority in the psychology of action.

14. Martin Buber, the Jewish mystic and social philosopher, has of course been most influential in recovering this Biblical anthropology for modern Christian thinking. See *I-Thou,* tr. by R. G. Smith (Edinburgh: T. & T. Clark, 1937), and *Between*

Man and Man, tr. by R. G. Smith (The Macmillan Company, 1948), or selections in *Four Existentialist Theologians,* ed. by Will Herberg (Doubleday & Company, Inc., 1958). See also Jacob Neusner, *Fellowship in Judaism* (London: Vallentine, Mitchell & Co., Ltd., 1963).

15. See Thomas Aquinas, *Summa Theologica,* I, qq. 75–89.

16. See *Rerum Novarum, Quadregessimo Anno,* and *Pacem in Terris,* in Anne Fremantle (ed.), *The Social Teachings of the Church* (Mentor Book, The New American Library, Inc., 1963), pp. 24–26, 84, 281.

17. The many sophisticated and subtle intricacies of Christian eschatology are here truncated and foreshortened for the purposes of quick exposition. Background material in more detail may be found in such standard treatments as Oscar Cullmann, *Christ and Time,* Revised Edition, tr. by Floyd V. Filson (The Westminster Press, 1954); E. C. Rust, *The Christian Understanding of History* (London: Lutterworth Press, 1947); Roger L. Shinn, *Christianity and the Problem of History* (Charles Scribner's Sons, 1953).

18. The bearing of Christian eschatology upon ethics has been a question currently revived in theological circles by Jürgen Moltmann, *The Theology of Hope,* tr. by J. W. Leitch (Harper & Row, Publishers, Inc., 1967), who makes the Christian hope for a real *eschaton* the ground of the quality of Christian faith and love.

II

The Ethical Qualities of Christian Community

Against the background of Christian theological affirmations reviewed in Chapter I, we now look to the foreground matters of the ethics of Christian community. This exercise is pursued on the assumption that ethics, as the science of the norms of human conduct, is always dependent on some ontological or theological base. Whether it be Christian ethics or any other, behind the description of the norms of right action, as their sanction, stand certain claims about the nature of the universe "out there" and the nature of man "in here." In Christian terms, the human moral imperatives rest upon the divine indicative: man's moral "oughts" find the answer to the final "why?" in the divine "is." In somewhat the same way, in certain versions of Greek ethics the ground of the moral command to "be reasonable" rests on the assumption that *Nous* (Reason) is the ultimate reality in the universe. So too the ethics of contemporary mass man, as surveyed by social science, is premised largely on the assumption of the ultimacy of society.

According to the interpretation here adopted, Christian ethics is the ethics of response. "Responsibility affirms—God is acting in all actions upon you. So respond to all actions upon you as to respond to his action."[1] This means that the morally good for Christian man is to be defined as action toward neighbor, self, and nature,[2] fitted to the divine action toward man. The inclusive "form" of Christian response in action is "to do the will of God." The contours of that will are understood in the categories of God's creating, judging, and redeeming activity, particularly as that is seen through the prism of Jesus Christ. How man responds to these modes in God's Kingdom, the ultimate "context" of his life, constitutes the definition of the ethical qualities of his earthly community.

Love as the Bond of Community

The whole thesis of this chapter, and indeed of this volume, can be put into a sentence: Love is the single bond of community. But this says nothing unless one goes immediately on to delineate the Christian meaning of love and to distinguish it from the other meanings of the term.[3] It is a word that has undergone many convolutions of meaning in the history of Western thought. In modern parlance, the single English word, "love," has to carry the freight of many disparate meanings. Love means physical or sexual attraction, friendship, admiration, sympathy, patriotism, pity, reverence, likeness of tastes. The common denominator in these various meanings is some kind of positive affinity of one person for another person or thing. To make true sense out of the semantic slough, the crucial matter is to look not to the word itself, but to the implicit or explicit context, the ultimate referent, for the sake of which the self is attracted to the object of love. A boy and a girl say they are "in love": the ultimate referent here may be a libidinal or romantic one. The love of friendship (*philia*) is a mutuality that finds its ultimate referent in shared delights and outlooks and tasks that hold friends together.

The subjective quality of love, then, all depends on its direction as that is determined by its last object, the context of faith within which the other is regarded and treated. There is always some middle term between the lover and the beloved. I may love the neighbor "in" or "for" some shared enthusiasm or enterprise: we are made friends in this common "field of force." The middle term may be rationality, or partisan politics, or sensuality, or Mammon. Or it may be egocentricity, in which the ultimacy of the ego itself is the final referent for the sake of whom the other is loved, where I love the other for myself supremely. Whatever it be, this middle term constitutes the distinguishing color and style of the actions of neighbor love.

It is plain, furthermore, that all human selves, as with human societies, are a mixture of loves, with many plural loyalties mixed even in an apparently single "loving" decision. Dissection of the anatomy of a romance—if it were possible to probe without dispelling its magic—would reveal not single but plural referents. In any given instance of patriotism, the love of country may prove a complex thing: fidelity to universal values may be mixed with nationalistic pride. As human selves are ambiguous in motivations, so human communities are polytheistic in their bases.

The empirical mixture which constitutes all living selves and communities does not annul, however, the premise affirmed in the last chapter of a voluntaristic view of man and society: a man is as he loves, and a community is as it loves.

The Love of God the Basis of Christian Community

A delineating adjective is needed, therefore, to distinguish the love that marks the presence of the Christian community within the others. Christian love is theocentric, or theonomous. It is differentiated from its close replicas and near facsimiles by the fact that God is the middle term between man and man, the One for the sake of whom the other is regarded. Kierkegaard put it cryptically: "In earthly love and friendship partiality is the middle term. In [Christian] love to the neighbor, God is the middle term; if you love God above all else, then you also love your neighbor and in your neighbor every man."[4] It is by reference to no limited or partial center of value that Christian love cherishes the other and makes its decisions about the other; not the state, or the church, or sex, or the economy, or even humanity—though inevitably love must be expressed through these impinging circles. When it is in and for God alone love becomes authentically Christian. There are several terms here that may stand as synonyms: reverent, theonomous, theocentric—"godly" is the usual adjective in Calvinism—or simply the term "love of God." Whatever the words, here is the grand axiom, the major premise of contemporary Christian thinking about community.[5]

As theocentric, Christian love is at root different from such humanistic love as would regard the neighbor under the aspect of humanity, in which mankind is the final referent. Such a humanism is often ably championed in contemporary thought to supplant what is taken to be an intellectually incredible apparatus of Christian theology.[6] Sometimes this is advanced as the true reading of the original ethics of Jesus (to be salvaged out from under the theological superstructure of Paul and the early church).[7] There is a genuine note of authenticity in this secular humanism. It corrects any kind of love so preoccupied in ardor for God as not to see the flesh-and-blood neighbor standing there in need. In the prophetic strand of Biblical ethics, authentic love for God and worship acceptable to him always entails deeds of service and concern for the community. The radical monotheism of the prophets is the basis of this invective against the divorce of worship from service and theology from ethics. The two parts of the great commandment are inseparable. In this spirit, contemporary Christian theologians sometimes define the content of the will of God in some such terms as "whatever keeps human life human."[8] In this sense, prophetic ethics is fully humanistic. But its humanism is derived and not ultimate: the final referent and ground of its moral norms it finds given not in human nature as such but in the cosmic Will at the heart of the universe that creates human nature to be what it is and redeems man's life from destruction.

Responsible Love

The theocentric referent of love is caught in the key term we will employ normatively to delineate Christian love: *responsible.* Other delineating terms often used, "faithful" love, or "obedient" love, approximate but cannot quite convey the subtlety of meaning in the word "responsibility." This term has become the leitmotiv of much contemporary Christian ethical analysis and reflection.[9]

Both the "vertical" and the "horizontal" dimensions of the Christian life are carried in the term "responsible love." Christian love is responsible *to* God *for* neighbor. The vertical dimension is the sense of ultimate accountability to the One who puts before one man the needs of another and makes him unavoidably his keeper.

The sense of accountability in responsibility presumes of course a freedom of choice, not an arbitrary freedom, but a freedom answerable in its choices to One beyond the neighbor. Such Biblical phrases as "the fear of the Lord," with its sense of the holy, the awesome, the numinous, gives to responsibility a crucial urgency, the sanction of promise or dread, the ultimate options of "blessing and curse, life and death" that loom in even the most menial daily choice. When set under the aspect of eternity, the choices of the moral life become profoundly serious.

Responsibility *to* God means responsibility *for* neighbor. Stewardship along the horizontal plane is compounded of gratitude and obligation. In gratitude I receive the other as gift—just as he is, this living person at my door, in my office, this walking bundle of creature needs, of unique traits and winsome charms, of unrealized potential. In love, I accept and cherish him as precious in God's sight. But also as steward I am obliged to seek in all my actions toward him the fulfillment of what he *ought* to become under God. His "ought," his "might be" may be at odds with his "is." Love as responsibility requires me to serve his real good, his "becoming," which may not coincide with his present desires. Here is the note of stringency in the responsible love of a teacher for student, of a parent for child, of a judge for a juvenile delinquent, of a voter for his citizenry, of a road boss for the men on his crew.

Responsible love is therefore to be distinguished from anomic permissiveness, indiscriminately accepting and indulging the other with no sensitivity to the distance between the neighbor's "is" and "ought to be." On the other hand, responsible love is not imperious, imposing its own image of the good on the other, insisting on community only on terms of the self's own righteousness. Moral imperialism is a peril that lurks very close to the exercise of responsible love in practice. The lover may dominate the beloved out of too anxious and scrupulous a care, seeking to stamp the self's own image on the other. Mother love becomes smother love. The lover preempts the prestige of God. Responsibility *under* God, on the other hand, gives love its genius and integrity. From it springs both acceptance and correction, both forgiveness and discipline.

The point is aptly put by Clyde Holbrook: "[Personal community] is a fellowship of free selves where the selves are bound together by common concerns and purposes, so that there is a maximum of joyful mutual acceptance and a maximum of serious judgment. Without the full acceptance of the other, we would have only carping criticism; without judgment and discrimination in respect to the other, we would have only sentimental alliance. . . . Only in love are we free to judge each other and to accept the judgment of another without rankling memory; thus love becomes responsible. We are free to forgive and be forgiven; thus responsibility is tempered with mercy and tenderness."[10]

Responsible Love as Personal

Responsible love responds to the action of God by a concern for the personal worth of the neighbor as creature, in a universe wherein the fall even of a sparrow is known by the Creator. Christian love is "personal." The meaning of this word is difficult to convey to ears dulled by political and business talk about "the worth and dignity of the individual," or the "worth of persons" and "personalized" relations.

The clue to the Christian meaning of personal love is found in the distinction of Martin Buber between "I-it" and "I-thou," a contrast normative for many contemporary Christian ethical writers attempting to restore the meaning of "personal" love in a depersonalized world.[11]

Personal love sees the other first as a sacred, precious, distinct individual, never first as a "case" of whatever collective he represents, or as one digit in a set of digits. "Every man is an exception," said Kierkegaard. I see the other as separate, as distinct, with a unique name. The Biblical style of God's calling each creature by name is highly significant. In the relationships of authentic personal love, I know another, and he knows me, in terms of intimate trust and mutual sensitivity to the distinctive outlooks and foibles of the other. The impersonal relations of the system, in the I-it encounter, are external: I do not "know" the other, but I have "contact" with him, a touching only, an association without inner community. Even face-to-face relations in the system lack the depth and intimacy of self with self. In the personalized etiquette of suburbia, a gesture of tribute is unconsciously paid to this Biblical tradition, when people are at pains to call each other by name, even if they only be casual acquaintances.

Such an understanding of *agape* love is normatively put in the Bible: in the prophetic motif of concern for the stranger, the poor, the weak, the dispossessed; in the aphorisms and parables that inscribe the mind of Christ on the meaning of neighbor love; and in the fleeting records of his own stance and bearing, "the man for others," in the Pauline descriptions of love in I Corinthians, chapter 13, and elsewhere.

Personal Love and Social Policy

A baffling problem for contemporary Christian ethics is that of translating "personal" love from the single and man-to-man settings in which they are Biblically defined into the large-scale collective relations of social policy. How does love carry its personal concern into the world of systems? How do I cherish the precious worth of that particular man when the conditions of social exchange put each of us behind the walls of the collective and keep us apart, strangers and remote? How may I translate the personal concern of the Samaritan for the one victim of thieves to a social policy that treats many thieves, and the impersonal forces that produce the thieves, with the same personal intimacy? These are questions that haunt every attempt to frame a Christian social policy. The working premise here proposed (to be explored at length in subsequent chapters) is that the Christian ethic of personal love remains normative. It will not suffice to draw a sharp line between persons and systems, between love in the singular and loves in the plural, between intimate circles of concern, like the family, where love can be expressed, and the collective circles of "the orders," like the state, or the economy, where impersonal justice is the best that can be done. The intent of a single ethic here is to find the ways that the personal regard of responsible love can penetrate and infuse cultural systems and sustain the fabric of community within them all. It may prove necessary, as will become evident, to exchange the ethic of I-thou personal love into the currency of justice as one moves from unilateral to multilateral neighbor relations, but love yet remains the regulative norm for a just social policy.

The theocentric regard for individual persons should not be confused, however, with *individualism.* In a good deal of popular evangelical Protestant ethics, with its habit of thinking of souls saved one by one, the notion of the "dignity and worth of the individual" is taken as pious warrant for a privatized ethic. I-thinking supplants we-thinking. Personal concern is honored in criticism of the exercise of corporate responsibility on the part of the government to affect the common good. Christian love is identified with a laissez-faire economic policy, threatened by statism or any collective, whether that be seen as communism or creeping socialism.

By contrast, the personal concern in responsible love is not individualistic. Classical Protestant moral theory has consistently affirmed the *koinonia* ethic, in the Biblical organismic style, wherein each is interdependent with each in the body of Christ.[12] "Communitarian," or "solidaristic," are the terms used in Roman Catholic moral theory. Its concern is for the common good. By natural law, according to Roman Catholic tradition, the worth of persons is seen as related directly to private property, but private property is always to be exercised for the common good. Here is the ground of contemporary Catholic support of land reform in Latin America, for example, and for governmental intervention in economic policy.[13] So too the ecumenical movement defines the Responsible Society as one wherein the concern for the worth of persons, especially the victims of imbalances in economic power, justifies the support of political measures of the "welfare state" to achieve larger economic equality of opportunity.[14]

Truthtelling in Responsible Love

There is yet another facet of responsible love in community conveyed in the word "personal." In the I-thou encounters, persons speak the truth to each other in love. Their relations are open and honest. In contrast to the I-it relations required by the "system," where the self is engaged in role-playing and mask-wearing, in many deceits and disguises, in all the dissembling gambits required by the game of public relations, the personal relations in authentic community are maskless: persons trust each other, in their truth-seeking and truth-speaking, in their speech and in their silence, since they are ultimately responsible for each other to One who sees in secret, and to whom all hearts are open. In the Gospels, the sincerity Jesus enjoins upon his disciples, in contrast to the hypocrisy of the Pharisees in their conspicuous piety, is a spontaneous and natural result of theocentric love. How ridiculous become social status-seeking and game-playing if it is only before the Lord that we are accountable and justified. The pretense of the Pharisees is valid if the Crowd is the ultimate arbiter ("Truly, . . . they have their reward"), but the integrity of authentic, truthful relations rests on an accountability to the Lord beyond the crowd.

This matter holds good in the relations of men as students of their universe and as neighbors to each other. For the scientist honesty is required in reporting on the nature of things by reason of his trust, and that of the scientific community, in the Faithfulness that permeates all things. And in communication among men, "You shall not bear false witness against your neighbor" becomes valid because of the covenant set by God, whose ways are one, loyalty to whom is the first of the commandments.[15]

The Dynamics of Community

At this point we may draw on an analogy from physics to describe the dynamics of Christian community, and say that it is common to all human associations, simple or complex, small or large, that they exist in some kind of equilibrium between two opposing impulses: the centrifugal drive "out" for individuality and separateness, and the centripetal drive "in" for cohesion and order. In the common life of a family, a healthy relationship obtains when the members go their separate ways and have their separate identities, yet where also there is a countervailing cohesive loyalty to the common good. The dynamics of a healthy political order are such as transcend both anarchy, where the centrifugal tendency is dominant, and tyranny, where the centripetal tendency is too great. Authentic community in the state is one protected from tyranny by a regard for individual rights and freedom, and from anarchy by a cohesive loyalty derived from a shared sense of loyalty to a common good, wherever that be centered.

This equilibrium between the centrifugal and centripetal impulses is not a 50-50 mechanical equipoise: here the analogy with physics as quantitative breaks off. It is always a dynamic, unstable quality of countervailing impulses expressing the wills of its members. Any one empirical community at any one time —like the monogamous American suburban family of the 1930's, or the court society of seventeenth-century France — would represent a complex mixture of these two polar opposite forces, with now the centrifugal drive and now the centripetal drive dominant. At any one moment there is a trend toward excess which prompts a counteracting trend. The human condition is like the shuttle movement of Schopenhauer's porcupines in wintertime, who huddle together to keep warm (centripetal), then separate to keep from prickling each other (centrifugal), and never quite realize the proximity of optimum community. History provides no illustration of a community where freedom and order have been perfectly joined. No family on earth has been a holy family, and no state a holy commonwealth.

As we have defined it above, the norm of responsible love becomes relevant in that it provides the dynamic for approximating the equilibrium of true community. Its exercise keeps community both from flying apart into anarchy and from tightening into tyranny.

On the one hand, love means loyalty to a common good transcendent of the self, a love that "seeketh not its own," is outgoing, disinterested in the self's advantage because passionately interested in a corporate good. As loyalty, responsible love provides the cohesive centripetal force in community.[16] The solidarity of the group depends upon such loyalty as its *esprit de corps*.

On the other hand, love as tolerance provides the opposite centrifugal impulse. This facet of personal love is sensitive to the individual differences of need, of talent, of conditions among the others about whom it must decide in action. "Tolerance" may be a word not quite adequate to convey the quality of personal love complementing loyalty. "Sensitivity" may be more apt to catch love's permissiveness and consideration. But whatever word be used, love on this hand fosters the individuality of the other. It seeks out the deviant and protects his right against the collective, if need be. Love as tolerance rejoices in the free play of individuality, in the richness of pluralism. At home, or in the marketplace, authentic community is not the identity of the same, but the bond of trust among the different. Love as loyalty sustains the fabric of community by actions furthering the interdependence of man with man. Love as tolerance sustains the richness of variety in community in all complementary differences. So it balances freedom and order, rights and duties, cohesion and separateness.

Responsibility in community, then, means love's correlation of rights and obligation in such fashion as that the particular empirical community does not fly apart into anarchy or submerge diversity into the collective, but lives in a relative equilibrium of a kind of spiritual *homeostasis*.

In the order of the family, for example, ideally speaking, the responsible love of husband and wife for each other and for their children may approximate community to a considerable degree. In loyalty to the common circle of the family, each will subordinate his private good to the common cause. Yet each will be alert to the special need of the other. A wise parent welcomes the centrifugal tendency in the rebel drive of his adolescent son to be prodigal, to veer from the father's expectations, to become an independent person out from under the parental authority. This usually is accompanied by turmoil and tension. The domestic tranquillity of placid community may be disrupted at one level, while responsible community may be realized at another.

The problem of correlating rights and duties in the political economy, as will be examined later, is a much more complex issue. But responsible love, though it may be only obliquely expressed in policy, is a norm no less relevant. In all the complex power structures that make up man's political life, from the P.T.A. committee to the United Nations, an equilibrium balancing the freedom of the parts with the order of the whole is the normative quality of community. The outer and visible terms of charter and constitution do not in themselves create community; they give expression to the inner and invisible *élan* or morale that sustains its parlous balance.

Equality and Inequality in Christian Community

Still another dialectic problem in the achievement of community has to do with the balancing of the norms of equality and inequality. Which of these shall be the rule of the house, or if neither one exclusively, in what proportions should they be mixed?

On this issue, traditional Christian ethical theory has been strongly hierarchical. Whether in the patriarchal or monarchical idioms of the Bible, or the feudal idiom of medieval thought,[17] the prejudice is strong in Christian history for the axiom of hierarchy, fixed ranks of higher and lower, inequalities of social station. More recently, this conservative tradition has been challenged by the democratic revolutions from an opposite bias for radical equality. In many instances, of course, these revolutions overthrew some entrenched power structure in which the Christian church had a vested interest, in the name of democracy against Christianity. In the course of Christian history in the West, however, an absolute identification of Christianity with either the forces of reaction or the forces of revolution is a bad distortion of the evidence. Christianity has appeared in both revolutions and counterrevolutions as champion of both new and old orders.[18]

If the historical conclusion remains clouded, the moral analysis of the matter is relatively clear: both equality and inequality are mixed in Christian community. To speak more precisely, true community is a mixture of primal equality derived from the shared creaturehood of all with the proper inequality derived from the given diversity of function. It is responsible love, as earlier defined, that rightly mixes the two.

Certainly a prime ingredient in true community is the will to equality. Responsible love drives toward equality in the body politic, for in response to God the creator, it sees the neighbor, like or unlike, stranger or friend, first as creature sharing a sacredness and a common dignity with oneself and thus deserving equal treatment.

But equality is only one pole of the dialectic. A quantitative equity, as the single rule of social policy, requiring the same from all and giving the same to all, would deny community, flattening out the richness of its diversity to a dead level. In the commerce of relationships in family, neighborhood, economy, and state, the "others" never confront me as the same, but as different, in a bewildering manifold of inequalities of need, talent, merit, seniority, achievement—all incommensurate by any calculus. The inequalities are as "given" as the equality. Even in the comparatively simple relations of family life, as a father I am confronted by plural demands that converge in my crucible of choice: children of differing ages make incomparable requests, the needs of my wife versus my own, etc. To close my eyes and prescribe the same for all would deny community in this household. To treat dissimilar cases similarly would violate what responsible love requires. Concern for the common good treats unlike cases unequally, with a love alert to the manifold individual deviations. The elder brother is a figure not confined to the Biblical parable. So, too, in greatly more complex form, responsible love prescribes a careful mixture of equality and inequality in labor contracts, in income tax laws, and the participation of European nations in the Common Market.

But what mixes the two rightly? The norm is that of "proportional" justice as the expression in action of a love responsible both to the equality of creaturehood and to the inequalities of the situation.[19] Roman Catholic social policy has spelled out the import of proportional justice for a variety of vexing social issues. In economic policy, for example, the natural law principle is that of private property for common use. Radical equalitarianism in possession and control of property is rejected[20] and centers of economic power and initiative are recognized as natural and right.[21] But economic privilege is relative to responsibility to the common good. Where radical inequities of land and possessions despoil the poor, the ethical mandate is for wider distribution of economic resources to close the gap between the haves and the have-nots.[22] Such an ethic, balancing equality and inequality in dynamic equilibrium, reflects the spirit of the Hebrew prophets. Nathan, Amos, Isaiah—and many another prophet since—grant inequities of economic power: there are landlords and there are people; there are kings and there are subjects. Yet as under the heavenly King, the prophets champion the cause of the weak and the poor in the name of corporate responsibility and challenge any, however mighty on earth, who abuse it.

A justice proportioned to responsible love maintains the fabric of community. The inequities "given" within all living communities, the authority of father over son, of employer over employee, of officer over citizen, are the occasion for justice where the greater privilege is exercised responsibly. "To whom much is given, of him will much be required" is an apt Christian aphorism.

The demonic perversion of community, on the other hand,

takes place when inequality is proportioned to the sin of self-will. Unequal decision or policy expresses a pride or partiality based on self-will, demanding greater privileges by reference to superior rank, setting the terms of community relations, of inclusion or exclusion, of rank or station by reference to wealth or skin color, family or national origin. Sometimes these accidental differences are even rationalized as divinely ordained. The consequences inevitably are broken community, radical inequalities, the scorn of the powerful laced with fear, set against the resentment of the powerless, and the makings of destructive revolution.

The Dialectic of Peace and Justice

This last matter suggests a further quality in community nurtured by responsible love: the equilibrium between peace and justice. As with equality and inequality, the matter can best be understood dialectically.

There can hardly be quarrel with a plain first point: that Christian community is peaceful. In the great discourses of classical Christian ethical theory, from the herald angels and Gospel beatitudes, through Augustine's *City of God,* through Calvin and Jonathan Edwards, down through such an encyclical as *Pacem in Terris,* the same cry is echoed: Peace on earth, good will among men. The peace here celebrated and enjoined upon men means concord, harmony, the mutual accord of all the members in a concert of wills. "The peace of all things is a well-disposed order,"[23] as Augustine phrases it. It is like Plato's *to dikaion,* or true justice, the harmony of all classes and groups in the state, each performing its function, staying in its appointed place. It means a condition beyond strife and contention, beyond wars and rumors of wars, where mutual trust and goodwill hold men in glad, peaceable community.

This is the authentic peace whose bond is responsible love, whose concord is a just harmony. In moral terms, it is radically different from a community whose peace is the false peace of injustice, where the peace is kept by the powerful to hold in subjection the powerless. For example, an industrial manager in the southern part of the United States may speak sincerely of his textile mill without a labor union as a "peaceful plant—we don't have any trouble here," as if this were the entire good of the matter. But the peace of this paternalism may hide the gross injustice of its wage scale. The pre-Civil War slave economy in America was "peaceful," for master and slave each knew and kept his superior or inferior place. But these do not represent Christian community, for their peace is the facade hiding injustice. It will not do to say then that peace, as simply the absence of dissension, is the sole paramount value in community, or that the Christian preserves peace at all costs. There are occasions when responsible love requires the breaking of a peace, in the name of a higher order and a common justice which the current peace prevents. Counter to the conservative ethic that cries, "Peace, peace," there is then the revolutionary ethic breaking through the peaceful facade, disrupting the old order in the name of a truer order. Christian community numbers in its fold, then, both peacemakers and peacebreakers, pacifists and nonpacifists, who share allegiance to responsible love beneath their differences. More than that, one Christian man may with integrity now be peacemaker and now peacebreaker, now conservative and now revolutionary, as guided by responsible love.

A debate of major significance in the ecumenical movement has to do with the relation of Christian ethics to revolution. In Roman Catholicism the question is being seriously probed as to the role of the church in the newly developing nations. Is the conservative spirit in its ethics of community so tied to the feudal age in which it took definitive shape as to make it intrinsically antirevolutionary? Or may the natural law be read to imply legitimate involvement of the church with radical movements of economic and political revolution, as in Latin America?[24] The debate is even more intense in Protestant circles. The Geneva Conference of the World Council of Churches (in 1966) sharply divided on this issue. Within the general consensus on the norms of the Responsible Society, there was intense dissension: Christians from the stable democracies of Europe and the

Americas who espoused social reform by orderly and constitutional processes found themselves set upon by Christians from the Third World and Latin America, who spoke for the need for revolutionary change of a drastic and violent sort, in some cases in cooperation with Marxists.[25]

Something of the same ethical problem appears in the dialectic between peace and justice in the civil rights movement in America.[26]

Clearly there is need for clarification of the place of the revolutionary ingredient in the Christian norm of community, as a mode of social change. Here the thesis is advanced that the value of peace bought at the price of an unjust order is to be counterposed with the value of justice bought at the price of disorder. Neither pole of this dialectic is to be taken as simply and solely good; both are subordinate to a "higher synthesis" of a just and responsible peace such as will never be realized in the harsh exigencies of history, but nonetheless the norm by which now peace is sought and now peace is broken. Or, to put it another way, in the compromises which make up inevitably the mixture of man's communities, responsible love is the norm by which in one case peace is compromised in the pursuit of justice, and in another case, justice is compromised in pursuit of peace. Christian community per se is not predisposed to revolutionary action, any more than to keeping the *status quo*. But when the cry for justice requires the disorder of revolution, it is justified in the name of a higher order and a more inclusive good than the good of the revolutionaries. Consciously or unconsciously, the Christian revolutionary remains thus faithful to the dictum of Augustine that men wage war not for its own sake, but for the transcendent good of true peace.[27]

The Freedom of Christian Community

Freedom is the final quality to be considered in the grouping of qualities that make up Christian community. It is a slippery, nomadic term, as erratically defined as it is universally extolled. Its integrity of meaning runs through political and economic rhetoric like a greased pig. Yet some quick shorthand definition of the concept is needed to fill out the definition of Christian community.

As with the other key terms of ethical discourse, freedom is a relational, or contextual, term: its meaning depends on its setting in action. To abstract the term from its context and speak of "freedom" by itself is meaningless, however viscerally appealing as a slogan.

The real clue is given by the prepositions "from" and "to." Freedom "from" means the absence of external restraint. The usage of the term here means that freedom "from" is a value or a good because the restraint escaped is alien or inhibiting. It is this first meaning of the word that is generally assumed in common parlance. "I am a free man" means that I am out from under anyone's domination. "Nobody can push me around." "We are a free people" means that we are not subject to foreign rule; we are self-governing. For shorthand purposes, we may call this the "American" meaning of freedom.

Another understanding of the term centers on the opposite preposition: "to" or "for." Freedom "to" may assume the condition of the active subject to be freed from alien restraint, but this is a vacant freedom unless the positive meaning is added. "Freedom is the power to do without restraint what is right and what one ought to do." (Goethe.) Psychologically, freedom "for" means the spontaneity of uninhibited positive movement of the self toward its self-appointed goals. It is not the absence of restraint, but inner propulsion. A "free" man is not an undetermined self, in this sense, but self-governing. It is an idea caught in Robert Frost's definition of freedom: "working easy in harness." By the same token, politically it means a community obedient in action to its ideals and governing itself accordingly. Without this freedom "for," the freedom "from" in action is tantamount to anarchy, the paralysis of inactivity. Freedom "from," by itself, is *anomie*.

It is for this reason that Christian ethical discourse subsumes freedom to responsibility. It is not the "Free Society" but the "Responsible Society" which is the normative term. As the

World Council of Churches defined the term: "A responsible society is one where freedom is the freedom of men who acknowledge responsibility to justice and public order and where those who hold political authority or economic power are responsible for its exercise to God and to the people whose welfare is affected by it."[28] Similar statements may be found in papal encyclicals and the documents of the ecumenical councils of the Roman Church. Permeating the explications of the details of the responsible society in family, political, and economic matters is the recurring theme: freedom and order are polar terms both to be sustained by responsible love, keeping community in equilibrium between the excesses of anarchy and tyranny. The freedom of the Christian society, then, is the fruit of responsible love. It is the corporate expression of what Luther put in famous phrases: "A Christian man is a perfectly free lord of all, subject to none. A Christian man is a perfectly dutiful servant of all, subject to all."[29]

NOTES

1. H. Richard Niebuhr, *The Responsible Self,* p. 126. The indebtedness of the author on this particular point—and indeed on all major concepts developed in these pages—to the thought of H. Richard Niebuhr will be manifest. See in particular his *Radical Monotheism and Western Culture* (Harper & Brothers, 1960) and *The Responsible Self.*

2. Responsibility to God for the realm of nature is a highly significant theme generally neglected in the current literature of Christian ethics. See Clyde Holbrook, *Faith and Community* (Harper & Brothers, 1959), pp. 113–120.

3. The literature on the various meanings of the word "love" in Western thought is vast. Denis de Rougement, *Love in the Western World* (Harcourt, Brace & Company, Inc., 1940), is a competent, if tendentious, interpretation. C. S. Lewis, *The Four Loves* (Harcourt, Brace & Company, Inc., 1960), is a lively, popular introduction to the issues. The classical Christian study is by the Lutheran theologian Anders Nygren, *Agape and Eros,* tr. by Philip S. Watson (The Westminster Press, 1953). Martin D'Arcy, *The Mind and Heart of Love* (Henry Holt & Company, Inc., 1947), Gerard Gilleman, *The Primacy of Charity in Moral Theology,* tr. by W. F. Ryan and A. Vachan (The Newman Press, 1961), and Robert Hazo, *The Idea of Love* (Frederick A. Praeger, Inc., Publishers, 1967), are three recent Roman Catholic studies. Reinhold Niebuhr's early *An Interpretation of Christian Ethics* (Harper & Brothers, 1935) and Paul Tillich's *Love, Power, and Justice* (Oxford University Press, 1954) are two influential Protestant treatments.

4. Søren Kierkegaard, *Works of Love,* tr. by David F. and Lillian M. Swenson (Princeton University Press, 1946), p. 48.

5. The convergence of Roman Catholic with Protestant ethical theory here is notable. The theistic premise of morality is reiterated in all the major modern encyclicals and in church councils (see, e.g., *Mater et Magistra,* pars. 208, 215; or Vatican II: *Pastoral Constitution on the Church in the Modern World,* par. 24). See Louis Janssens, "The Christian Concern for Society—A Roman Catholic View," in John C. Bennett (ed.), *Christian Social Ethics in a Changing World,* esp. pp. 166–172. This concurrence should not obscure the divergence on the matter of the original source and direction of *agape* love. In Roman Catholic—and to a large measure in Anglican—thought human love for God is "upward-moving." Nygren's classic study, anxious to defend the radical disparity between *agape* and *eros,* defines as *agape* only the inbreaking grace of God's love, discontinuous as much with Hebraic *nomos* as with Greek *eros.* Christian love according to Nygren at the human level is only that inspired by *agape* from God. The love *for* God he translates into the Pauline-Lutheran notion of *pistis.* Nygren's Pauline-Lutheran bias involves him in some contortion of the Hebraic elements in the gospel, for example, in his treatment of the Great Commandment (*Agape and Eros,* pp. 91–95). But all share the theistic premise and the axiom that human love arises out of the divine-human encounter.

6. See, for example, Erich Fromm, *Man for Himself* (Rinehart & Co., Inc., 1947), *The Sane Society* (Rinehart & Co., Inc., 1955), *The Art of Loving* (Harper & Brothers, 1956).

7. Some New Testament theology turned in this direction during the liberal era, e.g., E. F. Scott, *The Ethical Teachings of Jesus* (The Macmillan Company, 1924).

8. Paul Lehmann, *Ethics in a Christian Context* (Harper & Row, Publishers, Inc., 1963), p. 358. This note is reiterated in Dietrich Bonhoeffer. A major ethical work of Jacques Maritain is entitled *True Humanism* (Charles Scribner's Sons, 1938).

9. H. Richard Niebuhr's *The Responsible Self* represents his mature reflection on a theme that permeated his earlier writings. See Paul Ramsey (ed.), *Faith and Ethics: The Theology of H. Richard Niebuhr* (Harper & Brothers, 1957), pp. 140–146. A suggestive treatment of the theme is to be found in Walter Moberly, *Responsibility: The Concept in Psychology, in the Law, and in the Christian Faith* (The Seabury Press, Inc., 1956). See also Holbrook, *op. cit.,* Ch. VI. The theme of the Responsible Society, of course, is a dominant one in the ecumenical movement. See the essays by H. D. Wendland and Paul Abrecht in Bennett (ed.), *op. cit.,* and by James M. Gustavson in Egbert de Vries (ed.), *Man in Community.*

10. Holbrook, *op. cit.,* p. 130.

11. This profound concern for personal love is evident in many Christian theologians: Dietrich Bonhoeffer, Emil Brunner, Paul Tillich, Rudolf Bultmann, Nicolas Berdyaev; all are rightly termed "personalistic."

12. See, for example, Brunner, *Man in Revolt,* p. 290.

13. See *Mater et Magistra,* in Anne Fremantle (ed.), *The Social Teachings of the Church,* pp. 241, 244.

14. See the official report of the First Assembly of the World Council (Harper & Brothers, 1948), pp. 41–43; also Paul Abrecht, "The Development of Ecumenical Social Ethics," in Bennett (ed.), *op. cit.*

15. The bearing of this on the morality of science is discussed in H. Richard Niebuhr, *Radical Monotheism and Western Culture,* pp. 134 ff.

16. "Loyalty" is a key term in the social philosophy of Josiah Royce, whose theory of community is recalled in the later writings of H. Richard Niebuhr. See Josiah Royce, *The Philosophy of Loyalty* (The Macmillan Company, 1908), *The Problem of Christianity* (The Macmillan Company, 1913), *The Hope of the Great Community* (The Macmillan Company, 1916); also Stuart G. Brown (ed.), *The Social Philosophy of Josiah Royce* (Syracuse University Press, 1950); and H. Richard Niebuhr, *The Responsible Self.*

17. Cf. Otto von Gierke, *Political Theories of the Middle Ages,* tr. by F. W. Maitland (London: Cambridge University Press, 1900).

18. On this much debated historical point, it is important to distinguish between Christianity and the institutional church: they may appear on opposite sides of a revolution. The case has often been made that radical Calvinism was at the heart of the seventeenth-century revolution in England and America. (See James Hastings Nichols, *Democracy and the Churches* (The Westminster Press, 1951.) The relation of Roman Catholic and to socialistic revolutions in Europe and Latin America is highly ambiguous. (Z. K. Matthews [ed.], *Responsible Government in a Revolutionary Age* [Association Press, 1966].)

19. The term "proportional justice" is derived from Roman Catholic moral theory (cf. Thomas Slater, *Manual of Moral Theology* [Benziger Brothers, 1909]) and many of the papal encyclicals. It is similar to what is intended in Paul Tillich's concept of "creative" justice (cf. *Love, Power, and Justice,* pp. 64–66), and Reinhold Niebuhr's concept of "imaginative" justice (see *Nature and Destiny of Man,* Vol. II, Ch. 9; *The Self and the Dramas of History* [Charles Scribner's Sons, 1955], Ch. 21 on "Property, Social Hierarchy and the Problem of Justice"; also *Love and Justice,* ed. by D. B. Robertson [The Westminster Press, 1957]).

20. See *Rerum Novarum,* in Anne Fremantle (ed.), *op. cit.,* pp. 22–23.

21. See *Pacem in Terris,* in Fremantle (ed.), *op. cit.,* pp. 286–287.

22. See *Mater et Magistra,* in Fremantle (ed.), *op. cit.,* pp. 252–255, and *Constitution on the Church in the World,* in Walter M. Abbott, S. J. (ed.), *The Documents of Vatican II* (Association Press, 1966), pp. 280–281.

23. Augustine, *The City of God,* tr. by Marcus Dods (Modern Library, Inc., 1950), XIX. xiii.

24. See Abbott (ed.), *The Documents of Vatican II,* pp. 282–289.

25. See Bennett (ed.), *op. cit.,* who notes in his concluding estimate: "The most telling criticism of the adequacy of the concept of 'the responsible society' is that it reflects the older and more stable constitutional societies and that it does not fit the context of nations for which order and unity are priorities or nations that must first go through a period of revolution in which socially transforming justice has priority over freedom" (p. 379). See Matthews (ed.), *op. cit.,* also the official report of the Geneva Conference, entitled *Christians in the Technical and Social Revolutions of Our Time,* World Conference on Church and Society, especially pp. 96–119.

26. See Chapter VIII, below.

27. Augustine, *The City of God,* XIX. xii.

28. First Assembly of the World Council of Churches: Official Report, Amsterdam, (Harper & Brothers, 1948), p. 77. *The Evanston Report: The Second Assembly of the World Council of Churches 1954* (Harper & Brothers, 1955), p. 113.

29. See Martin Luther, *On Christian Liberty,* in *Three Treatises,* tr. by C. M. Jacobs, A. T. W. Steinhaeuser, and W. A. Lambert (Muhlenberg Press, 1947), p. 251.

III

Christian Community Between Law and Grace

What we have set forth in the previous chapter is an outline of the normative ethical qualities of Christian community in the order of creation. Let us recall for the moment what has been spelled out in detail: its bond is a love responsible to God and thereby for man in such fashion that persons are cherished, that equality and inequality, peace and justice, freedom and order, are balanced in dynamic equilibrium. It is the archetypal society, the pattern of perfection. It is normative in the sense that it becomes the criterion of judgment against which every particular present empirical social institution is to be measured for its moral worth. To put the matter "existentially," when I ask how good, in a Christian sense, the present condition of my life is, I lay this archetype against the quality of relations prevailing in the life of my family, or in my neighborhood, or in my state government. I can then answer the question of its moral worth with some degree of integrity, by reference to a criterion beyond such immediate ones as "It seems to work best," or "I like it," or "The people want it." It is also normative as criterion for judging the merit of projected goals in the future—such as for the "Great Society." In the temporal sense, it stands in my remembered past, as the original "given" order; it stands over the present societies, as the criterion of their worth; and it looms in the future as a goal toward which in hope I strive in my decisions and choices.

But in the Christian understanding of life, action must be taken in the light of other contexts and goals than this order of perfect community. For in the "fallen" world, east of Eden, I encounter my neighbor not only as good creature of sacred worth, but as sinner, as aggressor, as thief, vicious and prideful, whose hand is set against me. This prevails as much in private as in public affairs. In looking scrupulously within, beneath my self-defenses, I discover that I am a sinner also, a creature in contradiction, with a law in my members warring against a law in my mind, my own hand set against my neighbor. In this universal condition of the "fallen" world, I am required somehow to cope with this forbidding context of a disordered world and a twisted self.

We have spoken earlier[1] of negative community, to try to point to the limits set by the divine hand, in the activity of God as judge, who holds men in community despite their sin and prevents total disorder. It is that condition of the ordering of life that presumes self-seeking to be the mainspring of human action, and that sets a "dyke" against it, that man may dwell in at least the peace of armistice with his fellowman.

Good Fences Make Good Neighbors

The ethical qualities of negative community in the Fall are to be seen as inversions of the qualities of created community. It is a replica of the original created community in that at least it is an order where men abide by a mutually acknowledged *nomos,* the law of self-interest. In this there is carried the memory of the original mutuality of goodwill. But it is a negative replica in that its mutuality is based on distrust and animosity, not trust and love. Men are held *in* community, so to say, by being held off *from* each other. Their peace is the earthly suspicious peace of truce, not the heavenly peace of glad accord (to echo Augustine's categories of the two cities). Their law is the inversion of the Golden Rule: Do not do to another what you fear he might do to you. The universality of original community now appears in the common acknowledgment that all must abide by this law so that each may survive "the war of everyone against everyone."

The presence of negative community is readily evident in private and public affairs. The moral logic behind the green-andred light mechanism in city traffic movement is that one driver is held against his opposing driver coming the other way in order to obviate collision and allow both to get through. The folk wisdom of the New England aphorism "Good fences make good neighbors" is that community is better preserved when its members respect the limits set on the property—and acquisitive Yankee instinct—of each. In economic affairs, the commonweal is better served by systems of countervailing power, where one power bloc checks another, though to that extent the economy is a community of forced forbearance. In race relations, civil rights laws hold men together in open housing and desegregated use of public services, often in part against their aggressive prejudice for segregation. The most vivid illustration is in the international realm. Here the precarious measure of peace that prevails among the nuclear powers is not one based paramountly on universal goodwill. It is the negative peace of armistice, based as much on suspicion and fear, whose bond is the ethics of deterrence, the mutual trust that the self-interest of the other nation will not precipitate a breaking of the peace.

Life Under the Law

Considerably more than with Roman Catholic theory, Protestant ethical theory, rooted in Biblical categories, has paid close attention to this experience of negative community. Its point of departure has been the Pauline distinction between life "under the law" and life "in grace." In Martin Luther, negative community appears under the name of "the orders" of this world, such as the state and the economy, set by God's "left hand" to preserve civil life from anarchy, "as dykes against sin" and therefore to be obeyed as instruments of his justice.[2] In the Reformed tradition, the Christian's life is cast within the limits of such orders as the state, in order that he may achieve a relative degree of civil peace in this transient and troubled life. When Calvin argues that government should be "in the hands of many," rather than a single ruler, he does so on the basis of the "vice or imperfection of men,"[3] that each may restrain the other. So too in the economy, man is given a fixed post or station, partly in order to curb his wandering about in nomadic anarchy, and partly that he work out his experience of divine justification in home and marketplace.

The rule of the orders is the "sword," the symbol of coercion. In this life, the Christian is obliged as a citizen of the state to participate in its law-making and law-enforcing power, as soldier, as judge, as policeman. This is a dirty and brutal business, not consonant with the tender and gentle forgiveness of the Gospels. "A man who would venture to govern an entire community or the world with the gospel would be like a shepherd who should place in one fold wolves, lions, eagles, and sheep. The sheep would keep the peace, but they would not last long. The world cannot be ruled with a rosary," as Luther bluntly put it.[4] The citizen obedient to God in the negative community of the state must bear the sword for the restraint of evil.

Life in Grace

There is a third dimension of life in community, concurrent with the original order of creation and the fallen order of negative community: the community of grace. As recalled earlier, the crowning claim of the Christian faith is that the one God who brings the perfect order of creation into existence, and who guards it even in man's abuses and distortions of it through his structures of punishment in law, is also at work restoring it through the renewals of his grace. The gospel of Paul and of the early church in interpreting the significance of Christ's coming is a joyous faith in the recovery of a lost order and the restoration of right community: "God was in Christ reconciling the world to himself," and a confident hope in a final consummation.

The work of God in Christ is to establish after his name the "new creature" in the self and a new *koinonia,* drastically different in spirit from that of the world, though living squarely in it. It is to be a community of sinners who forgive each other because they have been forgiven by God in Christ. Those of this new community know themselves "justified" by God's grace, and restored into primally right relation to the source of their existence. They are freed from the essential sin of self-reliance and egocentricity, from a haunting anxiety and a paralysis of will, back into the confident freedom of spontaneity. This new freedom, however, is not lawlessness, *anomie,* but one that *fulfills* the law, does the truly lawful thing, no longer under the law as threat, or driven by it to gain status in the sight of God or access to heavenly reward, but as transcending the law, yet using it as a means through which to give love its concrete expression.

The ethics of grace on the human plane, as response to God's reconciliation of men with himself, is the will to resume community of man with neighbor where it has been broken off by sin. Its preconditions are contrition, non-self-defensiveness, and self-correction, for community broken by human prides cannot be recovered if the self continues to guard its I-castle. Responsible love as forgiveness breaks through all the fences and guards that are raised in negative community. It comes out from its I-castle openhanded. Love wills to resume community with the estranged other, whether forgiveness be reciprocated in kind or not. The moral worth of the ethics of forgiveness does not depend on its success in making friends out of enemies, though indeed it rejoices when enmity is transmuted. But the fellowship of reconciliation is *there* in intention, whether or not in fact mutuality is accomplished. Though its quality is determined by inward will, by its *intention* to resume community, its ethics is not privatized, but issues inevitably in resolute and tireless action making peace, proving neighbor to enemy and friend alike.[5] The fine distinction between the Christian ethics of forgiving love and the ethics of mutuality (*philia*) wherein one loves the lovable is suggested in Luther's comment that "a good man is more worthy to be loved than a bad one and that we are naturally more drawn to him, . . . but true love is independent of such external considerations, and it seeks out primarily not those who are most attractive, but those who are most in need."[6]

The Predicament of Ambiguity

The agonizing dilemmas for a Christian in his ethical choice often arise from the predicament that, though pledged and devoted to the original community of creation, his actual path of action runs between the community of law and the community of grace. In the traffic of this-worldly movement, he must reckon with the exigencies of negative community, obeying the coercive laws of the state, if need be, bearing the sword as himself a minister of its justice. In the marketplace, he must take part in its barter and bargaining in order to earn his living, with a shrewdness and cunning quite counter to the nonchalance of the birds of the air and the lilies of the field. At the same time, he is called in his loyalty to God in Christ to action that marks his membership in a community of grace not of this world. Even while he is engaged in the restraints and disciplines of law, he is called to forgive and minister in reconciliation to those whom he restrains. Even while he looks sharply to his own economic interests, he is moved by the compassion of the cross to a similar compassion and generosity to the very neighbor whom he has outdone or deprived.

In Christian history there have been many ways in which conscientiously Christians have wrestled with this ambiguity of existence between the demands of life under the law and life in grace, on the border between the two communities, to try to take some sort of stance of integrity between them. H. Richard Niebuhr's classic and familiar study *Christ and Culture* is a typology of five ways in which Christians have attempted to remain morally obedient to both, as disciples of Christ and creatures of the societies of the world.[7] Each of the five is an authentically Christian answer, but no one of them neatly or completely resolves the ambiguity. It is this polarity which is behind the issue perennially debated among Christians about the relation of love and justice. It is also behind the debates in the Puritan church over the covenant of law and the covenant of grace. Something of the same moral issue lies behind the differing theories of the nature of the church in the typology of Ernst Troeltsch, wherein the "sect-type" fellowship is one whose style of life is that of the pure community of grace, against the world, while the "church-type" church accommodates and compromises the pure ethics of the gospel to the exigencies of culture.[8]

It should be noted that the point of view informing the pages that follow is that the norm of responsible love, the law of the perfect order of community, can and does find partial, indirect expression within all the relative empirical structures of culture —the family, the economy, the nation, even the international sphere. This point of view (closely akin to the "Christ-transforming-culture" position delineated by Niebuhr) would maintain the *dialectic* relation of community under law and community in grace. It would drive between two extremes: (1) such radical dualism, sometimes associated with Lutheranism, as would divorce entirely the outer realms of the public orders from the inner realm of spirit and produce an ethic separating private love from public justice and (2) such a simple monism, sometimes associated with liberal Protestantism, as would hope to abolish the ambiguity by a progressive reform of communities of law into the communities of grace and bring heaven to earth. Christian realism would protest the latter course as expressing a confidence unwarranted by an honest look at history or current events. At the same time Christian realism, in a mood neither of despair nor of an undue hope for the future, in the name of God's sovereign rule over all of culture, and his unavoidable call to man to a life of responsible love, makes the claim that it is precisely within the ambiguities of the system and orders of culture that his will is to be done.

NOTES

1. See above, pp. 23–24.

2. Martin Luther, *On Civil Authority.* See William Mueller, *Church and State in Luther and Calvin* (Broadman Press, 1954), and Philip Watson, *Let God Be God* (Muhlenberg Press, 1949).

3. John Calvin, *Institutes of the Christian Religion,* IV. xx. 8.

4. Quoted in Roland Bainton, *Here I Stand: A Life of Martin Luther* (Abingdon-Cokesbury Press, 1950), p. 238.

5. The verb *gegonenai* in the Gospel parable of the good Samaritan is to the point: "Which of these three . . . *proved* [literally: seems to you to have become] neighbor to the man who fell among the robbers?" (Luke 10:36, italics added).

6. Luther, quoted in Watson, *op. cit.,* p. 137.

7. H. Richard Niebuhr, *Christ and Culture* (Harper & Brothers, 1951). The five categories are Christ against culture (illustrated by early monasticism); Christ above culture (medieval scholasticism); Christ and culture in paradox (Luther); Christ transforming culture (Calvinism); Christ of culture (liberal Protestantism).

8. Ernst Troeltsch, *The Social Teaching of the Christian Churches,* tr. by Olive Wyon (The Macmillan Company, 1931). Both Troeltsch's and Niebuhr's typology have proved productive hypotheses for the discipline of sociology of religion in interpreting the structures of ecclesiastical institutions as reflections of inner ethical dynamics.

IV

The Place of Values in the Social Sciences

Thus far we have attempted to resume dialogue between the Christian and the social scientist by recalling the main features of the Christian concept of community. As now we turn to the other party in the dialogue, to the student of contemporary society, we are asking chiefly: What are the generalizations and surmises made about the quality of contemporary culture that might resemble, or stand in contrast to, the Christian norms of good community? Before we can get to this substantive question we must reckon with the problem of *method*.

At first meeting, as we have already noted in Chapter I, the conversation might break off at the outset because of the prejudices and stereotypes, fixed furniture in the minds of both parties. One could hardly conceive of two more opposite positions than the position of the theologian and of the scientist, and the impression of each about the intellectual vocation of the other. The image of the sociologist may be that of "an aide-de-camp to an IBM machine."[1] The image of the theologian held by the journeyman sociologist is that of Bible-thumbing preacher or evangelist engaged in pious and vacuous daydreams about a heavenly kingdom. The theologian may pontificate from out of a closed dogmatic system and prescribe for any and all kinds of society the norms of the Christian commonwealth, definitively promulgated in Rome, Geneva, Canterbury, or Massachusetts Bay.

The rejoinder of the contemporary sociologist to such a parochial theological stance would be a quizzical puzzlement or a scornful disdain. From Auguste Comte on, the whole enterprise of sociology has been carried on, it would first appear, in declared independence from Christian theological preconceptions and ethical norms. Sociology is no longer—if ever indeed it were—subject to her majesty, queen theology, or to any world view, unless it be to Science itself. As such, sociology claims to be strictly descriptive. Prescription is not its proper task. As the conversation opens, the sociologist will declare outright as his *credo:* I am a student of human behavior in society, not an evangelist or moralist. I seek facts. I wish to describe society as it is, not prescribe what it ought to be, nor wail over what it fails to be. As a scientist I must remain rigorously empirical and objective, excluding all and any subjective value judgments. Amen.

Behind this commitment to what is usually called "scientific method" lies a considerable history and debate, much too involved even to summarize here.[2] It is a common impression that ever since Auguste Comte's *Positive Philosophy,* the direction of social science has been toward autonomy from any theological world view, along the road suggested by his three stages: theological, metaphysical, and positive. The nineteenth-century founding fathers of the "science of society"—Comte himself, Weber, Simmel, Marx, Durkheim, Spencer, Ward, etc.—though informed by many different philosophical slants and presuppositions, shared at least a common faith that as scientist the sociologist must forego all fancy and mythology, all tendential moralizing, and describe the face of society, warts and all, with clear-eyed realism. Max Weber's influential manifesto *The Methodology of the Social Sciences*[3] calls for the autonomy of social science from political as from ecclesiastical control, and a consistent distinction between fact judgments, the province of science, and value judgments, which cannot be derived from empirical science. Social science should be *wert-frei* (value-free). Though Weber recognizes the highly influential role played by human value judgments in determining social policy, he attempts—though with what success is a matter of considerable debate[4]—to keep the lines clear, insisting that valuations are extraneous to the enterprise of social science itself.

The emancipation of sociology from any Christian control

was furthered by developments in cultural anthropology. The study of the wide range of cultures, particularly primitive and non-Christian, revealed the almost infinite variety of religious forms and cultural institutions, of theologies and rites, of customs and mores. These findings ventilated the cozy assumption of Western European Christendom that the Christian structure of faith and ethics prevailed the world around. Cultural relativism blew to the winds any claim of Christianity to absolute universal and timeless validity. If one looked at the variety of moralities from the standpoint of a cultural anthropologist, such as Franz Boaz, Ruth Benedict, or Margaret Mead,[5] it seemed perfectly plain that there could be no universal transcultural vantage point from which to make comparative judgments about religious and moral systems. Christianity is only one among many. To claim any priority for its revelations would be an act of intellectual imperialism stemming from an ethnocentric parochialism hardly in keeping with the scientific spirit. Christian beliefs and values are not grounded in the nature of the universe, much less exclusively and infallibly true. Upon the close scrutiny by a cultural anthropologist like Sumner,[6] Christian morals proved to be not the timeless norms pronounced by the Son of God—but the mores of the bourgeois West, buttressed with the illusion of divine sanction. We are left with a complete moral relativism.

The empirical spirit in social analysis protests the futility of armchair theorizing about the nature of society. It is easy enough for a social philosopher, versed in his Aristotle or Thomas, his Jefferson or Locke, to ruminate on the condition of modern life, to squeeze its data into his a priori categories, and to spin out prescriptions of what its moral norms should be. But the effort proves an academic exercise in futility, entirely arid and remote from reality. What is needed rather are field studies, spot studies of particular societies where any a posteriori generalizations are drawn only out of correlations and composites of the data. The criterion of truth remains an empirical one: the cumulative quantitative generalization from the facts of how people behave toward each other, rather than logical consistency with a preconceived body of ideas. The vocation of the student of society is to "see through" the rhetoric and the ideology to the chaotic and raw stuff of human behavior behind the talk.[7]

The word "norm" does not mean, in this context, a moral good or value, a qualitative "ought," but some kind of mean or median average, statistically computed. If the political scientist makes the statement that A "ought" to vote Republican in this election, he means only that the voting behavior statistics gathered concerning the factors affecting A's choice point to a high statistical probability that he will vote Republican. The scientist is not admonishing or urging A to vote Republican because it is the morally preferable choice. In fact, as Robert Lynd wryly notes, the social scientist "prefers saying that 'ought' ought never to be used, except in saying that it ought never to be used."[8]

In a notable study of the history of the science of man, Floyd Matson[9] has shown persuasively how the social sciences have relied upon the quantitative categories of the physical sciences in their pictures of humanity. To the devotee of the "hard" sciences, the Christian theological premise about man as made in the image of God is incredible, since entirely unverifiable by any available quantitative measure. It has proved more rewarding to extend the method of the natural sciences from the study of inorganic and organic life to human life, on the assumption of continuity between man and nature, and the implied *dis*continuity of man with the transcendent or the divine. By this token, the quantifiable or measurable proves the real about man, as it does about stars and molecules. The qualitative categories used in traditional religious or philosophic descriptions of man, such as purpose, will, soul, aspiration, devotion, reasoning, prove so elusive to measurement as to be either discarded as unreal or reducible to physical matters that can be weighed and graphed. So human motivation can be explained, not internally by man's search for salvation, but externally by the S-R psychology of the salivating of Pavlov's dogs. "Theirs not to reason why; theirs but to quantify."[10]

Kenneth Boulding has remarked that ultimately there are two disciplines, poles apart, theology and mathematics, all others being admixtures in between.[11] We might put the matter in terms of a primal polarity between the qualitative and quantitative, between value and fact, between norm as ideal and norm as statistical average, between metaphysics and physics (in Aristotle's day next to each other, now poles apart). We might further say that insofar as mathematics proves the model discipline for sociology, expertise in social statistics becomes its crowning achievement and the Computer its King.

If the matter be left so, then dialogue would be futile. Daydreamers and Bible thumbers cannot talk with nose counters. All that ensues would be a continual argument, pitching the theoreticians, preachers, moralists, reformers, and idealists against the technicians and statisticians. (Some would claim that this is the main intramural contest played by the faculty teams of the contemporary university.) The theoreticians are dismissed by the scientists as "impressionists," balloon blowers, whose fancies can be quickly brought to earth when punctured by a single fact. In carrying their buckets of cards to the IBM computer, the scientists chant in chorus that statistics tell all, and that if the last survey did not quite catch the truth, the next one will, when we get a broader sample. The "impressionists" on the other side, refusing to speak in hushed tones before the Great Computer, point out in disdain that there is nothing more useless than an uninterpreted sociological fact, that the crucial criteria of "significance" and "meaning" cannot be caught in the however fine net of statistics, and that when posed with a simple moral question: How *ought* I to vote in this election? the computer—however suave in omniscience about the statistical probabilities of how I *will* vote—suffers a complete nervous breakdown.

The Revolution in Social Science

Fortunately for the cause of human self-understanding, the radical opposition we have described above is something of an outdated caricature. In fact, the major developments in sociological theory have been those breaking through this wall of separation between theology and social science, making possible a meeting of minds, at least on the terms of discourse, though by no means common conclusions about the nature of man and community.

There has in fact been a major revolution in the whole scientific enterprise that renders obsolete many of the nineteenth-century assumptions on which much twentieth-century behaviorist sociology continues to operate. The mechanistic models of the physicist, on which some quantitative studies of the social scientist are based, have been set aside in favor of newer models, wherein energy rather than matter is presumed as the basic datum.[12] The detached "objectivity" of the scientific observer, so long honored as sacred, has been definitively challenged, if not disestablished, by the thought of Michael Polanyi and many philosophers who follow him, as he has demonstrated the inevitable personal involvement and commitment of the observer in the process of scientific, "tacit" knowing.[13] The whole existentialist movement in philosophy is in one sense a protestant answer to the failure of objective science to catch the essential truth about man.[14] These have all resulted in a major revolution in sociological method.

Another real breakthrough coming from among social scientists themselves has been on the question of values.[15]

In addressing themselves directly to the value problem in social theory, and in transcending the "myth of a value-free sociology," as Alvin Gouldner phrases it,[16] social scientists have been brought back into speaking terms with Christian theologians. At least they can talk about ethics, if not theology. For to talk of values is to talk of what is good or bad, right or wrong for human beings in community.

Take again for the moment Boulding's polarity between theology on the one side, as the ultimate qualitative discipline, and mathematics on the other, as the ultimate quantitative discipline. It may make sense of the variety of the many different positions among contemporary social theorists to range them along a line or spectrum stretched between these poles, between objectivity and subjectivity, between outer fact and inner faith, that may give us a plausible typology of value theories among social theorists.

Starting from the objective side, we may discern a first position only a short distance away from sheer statistics. This would be a view acknowledging that the objects of study, namely persons in society, are not only digits, things, but also are valuing beings, who prize some things and despise others, and that therefore values constitute an unavoidable part of the data for study. Though the source of these values may be implicitly explained by reference to a Freudian, or Marxist, or Christian, or democratic world view, no attempt is made or implied, in this first position, to judge the validity of the values studied, or the ultimate truth of the faith system behind them. They are simply there, for good or ill, to be weighed, measured, correlated, graphed, computed in one or another quantitative way.[17] The discrete ethical distance of the observer is carefully maintained, however: no value preferences of the student himself are allowed to obtrude, whatever be his own personal commitment or persuasion,[18] though in fact they may obtrude in ways not evident to the researcher.

Perhaps another way to phrase this first position (or to spot another close by on the spectrum) would be based on a radical disjunction between means and ends. There are certain goals or ends of the good society, derived from men's moral insights and the historic tradition of the past: viz., a free society, a just society, a democratic society, a benevolent society. These are qualitative considerations, values taken for granted to start with. It is assumed that social policy should be turned toward these goals. The task of the social scientist is not to debate or judge these ends. Rather it is to discern and assess the strategies and means whereby social policy may be so framed as to implement these ends, to delineate not what is ideal, but what is possible and feasible under the circumstances. As Max Weber said: "An empirical science cannot tell anyone what he *should* do; but rather what he *can* do—and under certain circumstances what he wishes to do."[19] And the "circumstances" are the quantitative data of the structure of social institutions that impinge on human decision, the analysis of just how the machinery of corporate life works in its cause-effect, if-then sequences. These circumstances it is the business of sociology to describe, for the amelioration of social life through self-understanding.

In the area of race relations, for instance, the ethical goal of racial equality may be taken for granted. But the strategies for the movement of American society toward that goal require a close, hardheaded description of the cultural, legal, and institutional forces that condition racial behavior, including the dynamics of racial prejudice. The student of race relations may be said to be a moralist ultimately in his tacit allegiance to the moral end of a society of justice and equality and his hope for the amelioration of racial life. But proximately, he is value-free, detached, uncommitted, describing the stubborn, recalcitrant mores of racial behavior, whether he likes them or not.

The difficulty with this position is that it is not easy to separate means so cleanly from ends, or strategies from goals. "The ends pre-exist in the means" (Emerson), and the very circumstances or contexts of action are laden with value preferences.[20]

Another position farther along the spectrum would acknowledge, without apology, that the sociologist is moralist *and* scientist at once, not moralist at home and scientist at his desk, that there is a value-laden ingredient in the key qualitative concepts of social analysis, once it moves beneath the superficial level of sheer statistics.

For one thing, when one speaks of the integrity of the task of the social scientist, one implies a certain syndrome of moral qualities that constitute good scientific method. Rigor, exactitude, commitment to objectivity, accountability to data, loyalty to the cause of truth, coupled with intellectual openness, the willingness to alter or abandon old hypotheses in the face of upsetting new data, imagination and creativity in posing new hypotheses, faithfulness in reporting to others in the scientific community—these all are extrascientific values, a priori qualities taken for granted in the total vocation of the student of society, brought to the facts and not derived from them.[21]

But beyond this, and in a sense much more crucial for our

thesis, there are hidden or explicit value judgments made in the studies of social behavior—values not only in the stance of the student, but values honored and disvalues deplored in what he studies. Even in those field studies most apparently value-free, in the choice of areas of subject matter under scrutiny—race relations, urban poverty, juvenile delinquency—these problem areas are chosen as significant. But what is the criterion distinguishing the significant from the insignificant other than a moral one—that these are areas of social disorder, or social pathology? How may one speak, as now we do, of a "sick" society, without some implicit assumption of what constitutes health? And how may one intelligibly speak of disorder or dysfunction, without some implicit notion of good order or right functioning, in short, some moral axiom about community, that predisposes the selection of what is significant and relevant out of the larger hope that the disorder may better be corrected if its anatomy is carefully dissected and understood? If not a religious, here at least is certainly a humanitarian ethical concern running strongly between the lines of the descriptive enterprise itself.

This analysis has moved us considerably along the spectrum, away from a statistical, quantitative behaviorism. We now have crossed the great continental divide of methodology, from the domain of the quantitative to the domain of the qualitative. One methodological theme common to the most influential writers in contemporary social theory has been the use of key qualitative terms in interpreting the significance of the data. This is in no sense novel, incidentally, but a renewal of the *verstehen* method of classical German sociology. While on the one hand a Max Weber championed a value-free sociology, on the other, he espoused the necessity of insight, creative imagination, in the understanding of society. His disciples have been many. The newer generation of sociologists in England and America, refusing to surrender the field to the IBM machine, have in like spirit mounted a counteroffensive to behaviorism, insisting that the exercise of creative imagination is primary to the task of understanding society. There are qualitative a priori categories, "poetic metaphors" as Maurice Stein calls them, derived, one might say, from armchair reflection, in no sense the inevitable a posteriori conclusions derived from the quantitative cumulation of field evidence. They may prove more or less brilliant in their accuracy of impression when laid against the raw data.

The most notable advances in social analysis (as in physics or any of the natural sciences) have come about at the hands of a brilliant genius who has fixed on some key quality or syndrome of qualities that makes synoptic sense of mass behavior. Alienation, the lonely crowd, *anomie,* status-seeking, identity, role-playing, anonymity, atomization, rootlessness, organization man, etc.—these are highly poetic metaphors but for that no less accurate in capturing the *Zeitgeist*. They are terms that "catch hold," because they read the signs of the times. Their use leads Robert Nisbet to suggest that sociology may be called an "art form,"[22] an observation considerably unsettling to a statistician and quite baffling for the IBM machine to absorb and compute.

Perhaps the computer disciples will protest: If these key categories of social interpretation spring from the imaginative insight of the poet, are they not highly arbitrary and subjective? What happens to the criterion of objectivity so sacred in scientific method? How are the private insights of these "impressionists" to be publicly measured and tested? How can "alienation" be counted, and percentages of alienation correlated? It was the incidence of suicide in Western nations that led Émile Durkheim to his reflections on *anomie,* but not as a correlation of two commensurate variables.[23]

This delicate problem in sociological theory leads some social theorists to suggest that a radically different meaning of scientific "objectivity" is called for, namely, that true objectivity is the public revelation of one's basic subjective categories. The word "faith" may be appropriate to use here, meaning not blind credulity, but the primal assumption or hypothesis of interpretation. This entails not the repudiation of faith in the name of facts, but the articulation of the faiths that illumine the facts. As Werkmeister puts it: "Objectivity is achieved not by denying these valuations but by acknowledging them and stating them explicitly as integral parts of the projected research."[24]

Once this inevitable "faith" element is granted, the problem of verification becomes enormously complex (and far beyond the scope of our present endeavor or competence to discuss). In the strife of sociological systems, do we establish the claims of one poetic master metaphor against another by some aesthetic criterion? Is it judged true because of its graphic simplicity? Or by some historic rights of seniority, is it true because Plato employed it centuries ago? Hardly, though the recurrence of classical themes adds weight to their authenticity. No, in the last analysis, the poetry of the sociological imagination must remain ultimately accountable to the empirical data of social behavior. But how it may be checked out does not appear on the quantitative surface. The criterion of verifiability of key concepts is their power to catch the inner qualities or style of life of an age or a culture, as that style is existentially felt by the *total* person studying it sympathetically. The totality includes more than what can be quantitatively caught by the statistician: it includes the aesthetic, moral, and religious sensibilities and commitments, both of the student and of the society studied.

The Soteriology of Sociology

It is possible to detect yet another position still farther along the spectrum in the direction of theology. For there are some analysts of contemporary culture who not only recognize the crucial place of values, and interpret them from an explicit valuational standpoint, but who would go farther and advocate the adoption of certain ways of living as prescriptions for recovering the health of good community. After description, prescription; after diagnosis, remedy; after detachment, commitment. Now the sociologist becomes not only moralist, but in a certain sense evangelist, preacher, who offers his best conscientious answer to the question: "What shall we do to be saved?"[25] He presumes in his endeavor that there is a certain normative order of good community, that the present state of things in society can be analyzed as a disorder when measured against the norms of order, and that there is a possible better order toward which men might recover by taking thought and following certain courses of action. All of this involves a "religious" advocacy, a faith system, though indeed the "religion" explicit or implicit may be very different from the traditional Christianity of the churches.

There are quite understandable cultural reasons why sociologists demur from this description of their stance as "religious" or "Christian." In part this can be laid at the door of Christian thinkers themselves, who have misconstrued and privatized the meaning of theological categories.[26] Most contemporary sociologists find religious vocabulary foreign to their discipline. Yet, though in secular terms, they may be recovering authentic religious insights and be proclaiming a "saving" faith. This is "religious" in the sense that it has an implicit or explicit faith system about man in the total nature of things, derived extraneously from the facts (analogous, as we shall see, to the Christian view of the order of creation), a diagnosis of the dysfunctional ailments of contemporary culture (analogous to the Christian view of the fallen order of corruption), and a gospel of salvation in its faith that there is a better order than this present one achievable by human initiative and planning (analogous to the Christian order of grace and redemption).

At a later point we will take a close look at the values prescribed by social scientists for the recovery of community, as judged by the norms of Christian ethics. At this point it should be pinned down that there are high human values or "virtues," to use a more traditional term, urged upon man, pointing him to the way of salvation—the virtues of rationality (Maurice Stein), of autonomy from crowd control (David Riesman, William Whyte), of outgoing love (Erich Fromm) or "creative altruism" (Pitirim Sorokin). Or in the functional theory of a Talcott Parsons, where values play a most significant part as integrative of persons and cultures, surely an integrated self is preferred over a disintegrated one.[27] Integration is a clear parallel to the religious definition of salvation: to make whole.

In this treatment of the place of value in social science we have moved along our spectrum far from the value neutrality of statistics to the value commitments of a moral man studying his society with moral intent, in close analysis of the anatomy of its melancholy and openly avowing the ethical imperatives needed for its recovery of health.

But all this, he might break in to say, is still *ethics,* not theology. Why does God (especially the Christian God) have to be implicated? Must I be theologian as well as moralist? Must I don a robe? A Christian and a secular sociologist might talk together fruitfully of ethical values, but must we employ the theological superstructure of Christian theology as well? After all, protests the social scientist, the claim of a supernatural sanction for moral values can hardly stand secure when so plainly belief in the gods is the ideology of prescientific man sanctioning tribal values. In this emancipated day and age, the only plausible sanctions must be human, not divine. To insist that Christian ethics be grounded in Christian doctrine is an absurd anachronism.

A Christian rejoinder might be that the social theorist as moralist is—perhaps despite himself—yet a theologian, not in the sense that he subscribes to an official church creed but in the looser sense that beneath the values he espouses are certain large assumptions about the nature of man, history, and the character of the universe, assumptions that stand as the ground and sanction of his ethics.[28] These are the faith premises about the last reality, on which lesser modes of reality depend, or the Ultimate Good, to which lesser goods are referred when it is asked about them, "good for what?" When one pursues the question why reasoned behavior is better than irrational, or love better than hate, why the Nazi slaughter of the Jews was morally repulsive, why racial segregation is dehumanizing—such ethical questions, pursued to their last lairs, turn out to be theological. We use the term "theological" here in Tillich's manner: referring to the object of ultimate concern. Even though the answers may be given only in terms of intramundane or humanistic gods: the pragmatic god of functional order, or democracy, or capitalism, or dialectical materialism—natural or supernatural, hidden or revealed, the theological transempirical referent is unavoidably present.

The Nature of Human Nature

There is one crucial assumption about the nature of man shared by this new generation of social scientists: that man is radically different from the animal. The assumption of most earlier behavioristic sociological research was based, as we have noted, on the continuity between man and animal. This derived in part from the attraction of social scientists to the method of the natural sciences. A greater measure of certainty in describing man's behavior in society could be hoped for by making "downward comparisons" of man's herd behavior with animal herd behavior,[29] by analogies with measurable behavior of his primate cousins below him on the scale of creation. One is reminded of Robert Frost's rueful lines:

> Our worship, humor, conscientiousness
> Went long since to the dogs under the table
> And served us right for having instituted
> Downward comparisons. As long on earth
> As our comparisons were stoutly upward
> With gods and angels, we were men at least,
> But little lower than the gods and angels.
> But once comparisons were yielded downward,
> Once we began to see our images
> Reflected in the mud and even dust,
> 'Twas disillusion upon disillusion.
> We were lost piecemeal to the animals,
> Like people thrown out to delay the wolves.[30]

But in the new social science it is the *dis*continuity of man with nature that is definitive. In the anthropological assumptions brought to the study of man's behavior in the mass are explicit qualities of humanity: rationality, freedom, a capacity for deliberate self-conscious choice, aspirational, affiliative, and affectional needs that mark man off as unique. Counter to the reductionist tendency of earlier behaviorism, contemporary social psychology and cultural anthropology are more sensitive to what makes man a *high-grade* Simian than what he shares with his Simian ancestry, or with the termites. One writer says that man is a "social animal," but not as insects are:

> The social phenomena of the termite colony, for example, are based upon *instinct,* which positive science interprets as mechanism. Man is social as a feeling, knowing, thinking, desiring and acting *individual.* . . . Man is also a problem-solving entity at the higher level of critical deliberation about ends, or free choice of ends on the basis of thinking, illustrated by the pursuit of truth. That is, he is a being who seeks, and in a real sense creates, values. . . . In contrast with natural objects—even with the higher animals—man is unique in that he is dissatisfied with himself; he is the discontented animal, the romantic, argumentative, aspiring animal.[31]

What makes man in society humane is that he is a "relational being" (Berger), an affiliative creature, an intentional being, who craves a sense of significance in his existence. These concepts all put the sociologist in the same circle of discourse with the Christian thinker whose doctrine of human nature presumes the same discontinuity of man from animal. For it is a translation into secular language of the ancient Christian faith that man is created in the image of God, who finds the meaning of his existence in love.[32] This same shared high view of human nature prompts the deep moral concern of the urban sociologist about the dehumanization of life in the crush and turmoil of the city. His use of words like "brutalization" and "degradation" is a semantic sign of his passion that man should not live like "rats pell mell in the straw," as John Calvin said.

The Eschatological Dimension

A second theological assumption hidden in contemporary social theory has to do with the large axiom about the direction of history and human destiny. Though its scientific preoccupation with specific and local spot studies has closed off an interest in the long historical look (and fostered what might be called the myopia of contemporaneity), there is nonetheless a certain view of historical movement apparent at a close reading between the lines.

Much of nineteenth-century social philosophy and analysis took for granted a progressive and optimistic view of human history. The disciples of Comte, Spenser, Darwin, as well as of Marx and the utilitarians, anticipated the amelioration of human life by revolution or evolution, as men suddenly or gradually substituted for the superstitions and fetishes of primitive religion the technique of science in the control of their environment. All this on the grand assumption that the same techniques so brilliantly successful in the study of nature beneath him would be equally beneficial when applied to man's study of himself and his neighbor beside him. The overtone in the very distinction between "primitive" and "civilized" man presumed the axiom of progress.[33] Many social reform movements of the nineteenth and early twentieth centuries were sustained by this hope. Utopian promises were in the air, and many Utopian communities launched. Much of Christian thought, especially Protestant liberalism, was colored in its view of human destiny by this pervasive view of history as progress toward the Kingdom of God on earth.[34]

In the twentieth century, however, there has been a sharp change of mood from Utopian to what has been called by Chad Walsh "dystopian" expectations. Whereas the language of the business and the political community, at least in America, is still the language of hope and progress, of crusade and pilgrimage toward a better tomorrow, of advance on "new frontiers" toward the "Great Society," the mood of the cultural diagnosticians is one of profound concern. They are the prophets of doom or at least of crisis. The tone of voice is eschatological. Progress is out; crisis is in. Those who acknowledge explicitly the value of humanity—freedom, creativity, rationality, aesthetic sensitivity—see them threatened if not destroyed by the conditions of modern living. It is the "decline of the West," and its dark distempers, not its progress, that are most commonly remarked.

Take for example the title of a recent major synoptic study of several American community studies, *The Eclipse of Community.*[35] Maurice Stein summarizes his conclusions: the cumulative effect of urbanization, industrialization, bureaucratization has "eclipsed" man's authentic existence in community and left him with a feeling of shipwreck. This is the "paradise lost" theme, or what might be called "rural nostalgia." Presumably, before the city and the mass media killed man's spirit and produced collectivized automatons, there was some fine style of life lived back on the farm or in the friendly small town. There is a kind of inverted romanticism,[36] or "Currier and Ives illusion" infusing this and similar studies of the culture of cities. The perfect community is transplanted in time from the future to the past, and the present is seen as a kind of cultural skid row. Whether or not the prophets of progress or the prophets of decline are the more accurate as seers is not the matter to be settled here; the only point claimed is that the social scientist who avows certain human values becomes something of a philosopher of history, perhaps quite unwittingly, when he engages in surmises on the fate of these values in the crucible of history.

Not only does the valuation element in sociology infer a certain premise about human nature, and the historical direction of culture. It also entails assumptions about the nature of ultimate reality, or ontology. Now we have moved along the spectrum all the way to the other pole. The social scientist oriented toward statistics would not be happy even to be suspected of any submerged theological commitments. Yet there are hints of certain cosmic referents behind the value orientations we have uncovered.[37] As C. Wright Mills once observed, "Any style of empiricism involves a metaphysical choice—a choice as to what is most real."[38] Insofar as given to "downward comparisons" of man with the material, the implicit ontology is a materialistic one: the ultimate "stuff" of the universe is matter in motion, blind and purposeless. Insofar as given to "upward comparisons," the implicit ontology may be a spiritual one: the ultimate "stuff" of the universe is spirit which impels matter. The first presupposition may be a theistic one, or it may be a sheer nihilism. The last answer of faith's query about final meaning to the human enterprise may be a blank, a silence, an abyss, or it may be a positive yes, an affirmation of a One in the many, a single positive source of being and value. Such an ultimate presupposition Werkmeister affirms thus: "The rationale of science, however, and the requisite to ultimate objectivity, is the faith that, beyond our wishes and predilections, there is an order in the universe which, though but dimly perceived, is yet amenable to rational interpretation and a rational value analysis."[39] This last great choice, between meaning and meaninglessness, is an ontological choice unavoidable to one thoroughgoing in his description of society.

Again, no claim is made at this point, any more than with the issue of the nature of man and of history, that a theistic ontology must be true, and an atheistic one false. The only claim staked out is that true empiricism will require of the scientist both the technical competence of the statistician and the imaginative reflections of the moralist and theologian. He does not need to choose between "significance without exactness" and "exactness without significance." He may have both. If full-ranged sociological method includes both, then the cause of human self-understanding and the advancement of human community might be furthered if the warfare between statisticians and the impressionists were halted, their jealousies for exclusive omniscience put by, and each party carry on its conscientious work with a trust in the integrity of the other, and a shared consensus that both faith and facts are necessary to wisdom.

Christian Ethics and the Problem of Values

This analysis of the problem of values in social science might prompt some interesting rejoinders and reflections from the Christian theologian who is the other party to our dialogue. There prove to be many more common talking points than first appeared possible when the conversation opened.

There is a considerable body of literature in Christian ethics on value theory technically identified as such.[40] But in a broader sense, *all* Christian ethics is concerned with value theory, in that it deals with the nature and ground of the "good" or "goods" for man. In many ways, the debate we have reviewed about the legitimate place of values in the social sciences is not new, but a repetition in new categories and language of a perennial debate in Western thought, of the conversations of Socrates with the Sophists, of the collision of Christ with the Pharisees, of the medieval clash between nominalist and realist, the debates in British empiricism, and of Kant's reflections when he had been aroused from his dogmatic slumbers.

In recent philosophy much attention has been given to the issue as to the *locus* of values: whether they exist subjectively only, in the mind of the valuing persons, or objectively, with an existence independent of the value preferences of the subject.[41] Whatever clarification may come from this debate, the issue remains stalemated when put in this either-or form, with serious antinomies clinging to either the "subjective" or "objective" value position.

The position adopted in this volume is one that brackets the problem as traditionally put in the subjective-objective polarity. It proposes a resolution in a new way. H. Richard Niebuhr has set forth the main lines of this position in an essay, "The Center of Value."[42] It can be called "objective relativism," or more simply, a *relational* theory of value. Values are conceived not as a realm of "essences" independent of persons in community. Nor are they merely subjective preferences. They exist relationally, *for* persons in community. "Value is the *good-for-ness* of being for being in their reciprocity, their animosity, and their mutual aid. Value cannot be defined or intuited in itself, but everything has value, positive or negative, in its relations."[43]

Though the explication of this value theory is only sketched without detail, it suggests a resolution of the antinomy that clings to the traditional idealistic value theory, viz., that the realm of essence may be so remote, so depersonalized as to be valued for or by no one. On the other hand, the relational value theory would avoid the antimony haunting the subjective value theory, traditionally conceived, that if a value is the object of any subjective interest, and value judgments no more than emotional ejaculations, then there is no possible criterion for judging the merit of one value preference over another. A relational theory of value "agrees with the subjective value theory insofar as the latter regards value as relative to being, disagreeing, however, with the relativism which makes the good relative to desire rather than to need, or which makes it relative to man as absolute center of value."[44]

A Christian theory of value of the sort proposed may prove, on close examination, to be more congenial with the value theory implicit in the cultural analysis of the social scientist than with that of the philosopher, valuable as his reflection may be in refining thought. For both Christian ethicist and social scientist, values and disvalues, goods and bads, appear always in the matrix and traffic of social exchange, in the ways flesh-and-blood men deal with each other. For the Bible, as for the cultural anthropologist, they have a societal setting and origin. Both sociologist and Christian moralist concur at least in this: values are always and only goods for persons in community.

The relational view of value really transforms the question from the form in which it is traditionally cast. The issue for serious talk now becomes: What are the components in the community, or who are to be considered members of the community *for* whom values are good? Among the many societies converging in the individual: family, school, economic class, nation, church—societies all expecting his allegiance yet often colliding in value demands, never neatly nested in a series of concentric circles—in all this, *which* society becomes paramount? What ultimate loyalty or final allegiance decides the question of priority where loyalty to one society collides with another?

Here is where the Christian theologian must enter a demur as to the adequacy of that sort of functionalist value theory, so common in contemporary sociology, whose ethical formula says that the good is anything that enables the self to adjust or conform, and that enables the society to function harmoniously. Such a monolithic societal arbiter of value choices is quite too simple and naïve. It is self-evident that disruptive nonconformity, out of allegiance to higher values than the present established mores, may lead to better community. The criterion of proper functioning simply begs the question; it does not answer it. Society itself cannot arbitrate the merit of competing value claims arising within its own sectors.

The theologian may raise the same question in another way: How ecumenical is the concept of community presumed in one or another sociological theory? Is the society for whom values are determined as valid for its members a limited one, circumscribed by the nation-state, or the communist bloc, or the democratic West? There is a steady peril of ethnocentrism in such social analysis as identifies the good society with democracy, Western style. Or is the image of community a universal one, inclusive of mankind? A deeper and more probing question to be asked is, Not only how extensive, quantitatively speaking, is the society which is the ultimate referent for the good, but how inclusive qualitatively? Are we to be limited to the flat plane of human society, or is there a One transcendent of the mass, in the vertical or depth dimension of human existence, spoken of with the symbol God, loyalty to whose will is a determinative consideration in prescribing the good? The covenant community of Christian ethics, as we have seen, starts with the premise of a divine Power, who is the final referent of human values and goods. He is construed as more than a symbol for society, or "the Generalized Other." Nor is he construed as just another Person to be added to all the population who make up society. He is the supreme member of the total community. In the Hebrew-Christian faith, as Richard Niebuhr remarks, "its starting point . . . is with the transcendent One for whom alone there is an ultimate good and for whom, as the source and end of all things, whatever is, is good."[45]

At this point in our dialogic search for the norm of good community, this theocentric referent in human societies may introduce a note quite troublesome to the secular sociologist, an unmanageable and illicit hypothesis. To the defense of this theocentric claim we shall attend in the course of the next chapter.

This one we leave in the hope that theologian and social scientist have been brought at least into talking terms with each other about what must be taken into account in understanding community.

NOTES

1. Peter Berger, *Invitation to Sociology,* p. 8.

2. Of the many standard works that trace this story, one might cite Howard Becker and H. E. Barnes (eds.), *Social Thought from Lore to Science* (Dover Publications, Inc., 1961); H. E. Barnes, *An Introduction to the History of Sociology* (The University of Chicago Press, 1948).

3. Max Weber, *The Methodology of the Social Sciences.* The substance of the argument is contained in Maurice Natanson (ed.), *Philosophy of the Social Sciences,* pp. 355–418.

4. See Leo Strauss, "Natural Right and the Distinction Between Facts and Values," in Natanson (ed.), *op. cit.,* pp. 419–457. Also, Alvin W. Gouldner, "Anti-Minotaur: the Myth of a Value-Free Sociology," in Maurice R. Stein and Arthur J. Vidich (eds.), *Sociology on Trial.*

5. Ruth Benedict, *Patterns of Culture* (Houghton Mifflin Company, 1934); Margaret Mead, *Coming of Age in Samoa* (William Morrow and Company, Inc., 1928), *From the South Seas* (William Morrow and Company, Inc., 1939), *Male and Female* (William Morrow and Company, Inc., 1949). A closely reasoned Christian interpretation of the problem of relativism is found in J. V. Langmead Casserley, *Morals and Man in the Social Sciences* (London: Longmans, Green & Co., Ltd., 1951), Ch. 6. See also David Bidney, "Philosophical Presuppositions of Cultural Relativism and Cultural Absolutism," in Leo Ward (ed.), *Ethics and the Social Sciences* (University of Notre Dame Press, 1959).

6. William Graham Sumner, *Folkways* (Ginn and Company, 1907).

7. See Berger, *Invitation to Sociology,* Chs. 1 and 2.

8. Robert S. Lynd, *Knowledge for What?* (Princeton University Press, 1939), p. 180.

9. Floyd Matson, *The Broken Image* (George Braziller, Inc., 1964).

10. *Ibid.*, p. 93.

11. Kenneth Boulding: "One suspects sometimes that there are only two rational sciences, theology and mathematics, and that all differences arise from the first and all agreements from the second" (*The Organizational Revolution* [Harper & Brothers, 1953], p. 245). Maurice Natanson puts this polarity perhaps more accurately in his analysis of the two polar positions in the social sciences, the "objective" and "subjective" *Weltanschauungen* (*op. cit.*, p. viii). His excellent introduction to this volume of readings parallels closely the analysis of the present chapter.

12. Matson, *op. cit.*, p. 130.

13. Michael Polanyi, *Personal Knowledge*. See also his *Science, Faith and Society* (London: Oxford University Press, 1946).

14. Edward Tiryakian, *Sociologism and Existentialism.*

15. No attempt has been made in this study to do justice to all the extensive literature on the value question in social science (and the value problem lurks in many places where the terms "value" or "ethics" may not be used). The following works have proved of special pertinence, almost all of them written from a nontheological point of view: Howard Becker, *Through Values to Social Interpretation* (Duke University Press, 1950); Daniel Lerner (ed.), *The Human Meaning of the Social Sciences* (Meridian Books, Inc., 1959); William Kolb, "The Changing Prominence of Values in Modern Sociological Theory," in Howard Becker and Alvin Boskoff (eds.), *Modern Sociological Theory in Continuity and Change* (The Dryden Press, Inc., 1957), and many other articles; Ward (ed.), *op. cit.;* Lynd, *op. cit.;* Gunnar Myrdal, *Value in Social Theory* (Harper & Brothers, 1958); Maurice R. Stein, *The Eclipse of Community* (Princeton University Press, 1960), Epilogue; David Bidney, *Theoretical Anthropology* (Columbia University Press,

1953); C. Wright Mills, *The Sociological Imagination* (Oxford University Press, Inc., 1958); Helmut Schoeck and J. W. Wiggins (eds.), *Scientism and Values* (D. Van Nostrand Company, Inc., 1960), especially the essay by William H. Werkmeister; Frank H. Knight, "Fact and Value in Social Science," in Ruth Nanda Anshen (ed.), *Science and Man* (Harcourt, Brace and Company, 1942); Peter Berger, *Invitation to Sociology,* and *The Precarious Vision* (Doubleday & Company, Inc., 1961); Edward Tiryakian (ed.), *Sociological Theory, Values, and Sociocultural Change: Essays in Honor of Pitirim A. Sorokin* (The Free Press of Glencoe, Inc., 1963); Stein and Vidich (eds.), *op. cit.;* Robin Williams, *American Society* (Alfred A. Knopf, Inc., 1951, 2d ed. 1960); Gibson Winter, *Elements for a Social Ethic*. The value problem also of course pervades the writings of the older major figures, such as Durkheim, Tönnies, Mannheim, and Sorokin. One significant pamphlet calls for the distinctively Judeo-Christian approach in sociological method: Arnold S. Nash, *Sociology, Science and Theology,* in the Faith-Learning Studies, published by the Faculty Christian Fellowship, 475 Riverside Drive, New York, N.Y.

16. Gouldner, *loc. cit.,* pp. 35–53.

17. A classic instance of such quantification is Pitirim Sorokin's attempt to graph the differing proportions of ideational and sensate values in the history of Western civilization. See *Society, Culture and Personality* (Harper & Brothers, 1947), p. 612.

18. William H. Werkmeister's helpful three-way distinction between values *of* social science, values *in* social science, and values *for* social science (cf. Schoeck and Wiggins [eds.], *op. cit.,* pp. 4–19) clarifies this point. When Myrdal makes the claim that his study of race relations is a study *of* morals, not *in* morals (*Value in Social Theory,* p. 64), he seems to belong in this first position, though actually he belongs farther along the spectrum toward theology. The great number of studies of attitudes and behavior patterns that make up the bulk of advanced sociological research in American universities may be taken as representative of this first type.

19. Quoted in Natanson (ed.), *op. cit.*, p. 360.

20. Myrdal, *Value in Social Theory,* pp. xxi, 48–49. This means-ends distinction is also found in Lloyd Easton, "Science and Values," in Russell E. Bayliff, *et al., Values and Policy in American Society* (Wm. C. Brown Company Publishers, 1954), pp. 30 ff.

21. Cf. William H. Werkmeister, in Llewelyn Gross (ed.), *Symposium on Sociological Theory* (Row, Peterson & Company, 1959), and in Schoeck and Wiggins (eds.), *op. cit.*, pp. 6–7. Cf. H. Richard Niebuhr, *Radical Monotheism and Western Culture,* pp. 132 ff.

22. Robert Nisbet, "Sociology as an Art Form," in Stein and Vidich (eds.), *op. cit.*, pp. 148–161. A computer would be needed to catalog all the uses of poetic metaphors and the *verstehen* method in recent sociological literature. The key writers here are C. Wright Mills, especially *The Sociological Imagination;* Pitirim Sorokin, in his use of ideational vs. sensate orientations of culture; Robert Redfield, David Bidney, H. Stuart Hughes in *Consciousness and Society* (Alfred A. Knopf, Inc., 1958), who speaks of the method as "perspectivism"; J. Bronowski, *Science and Human Values* (Julian Messner, Inc., 1956); David Riesman, who analyzes in *The Lonely Crowd* (Yale University Press, 1950) the dynamics of American society by characterological orientation; Robin Williams, Gunnar Myrdal, Robert Merton, Peter Berger, William Whyte, as well as more philosophically-oriented social theorists, such as Erich Fromm, Lewis Mumford, Robert MacIver, and Walter Lippmann. The elaborate position of Talcott Parsons uses no simple key poetic motif, but his system certainly belongs within this general rubric. Robert Nisbet's *Sociological Tradition* (Basic Books, Inc., 1966) is one of the most thorough treatments of this issue at hand.

23. Émile Durkheim, *Suicide: A Study in Sociology,* tr. by John A. Spaulding and George Simpson (The Free Press of Glencoe, Inc., 1951).

24. William H. Werkmeister, "Theory Construction and the Problem of Objectivity," in Gross (ed.), *op. cit.*, p. 503. See also his *Philosophy of Science* (Harper & Brothers, 1940). The same point is affirmed by Weber, by Myrdal (*Value in Social Theory,* pp. xxvii, 152), by Frank Knight (*loc. cit.,* p. 344), by Robert K. Merton, *Social Theory and Social Structure* (The Free Press of Glencoe, Inc., 1949; rev. and enlarged 1957), and by C. Wright Mills (*The Sociological Imagination*).

25. It is interesting that the very title of George Lundberg's famous manifesto for an amoral approach to sociology *Can Science Save Us?* (Longmans, Green & Co., Inc., 1951), is itself value-laden: it presumes at least that salvation would be a good thing for us.

26. Robert Nisbet, *The Quest for Community* (Oxford University Press, Inc., 1953; reprinted as *Community and Power* [Galaxy Book, Oxford University Press, 1965]), notes a reversal from traditional Protestant individualism toward a strong concern for community in the present, p. 29.

27. See Kolb, *loc. cit.,* p. 115. Also Daniel Foss, "The World View of Talcott Parsons," in Stein and Vidich (eds.), *op. cit.,* pp. 96–127.

28. See Nash, *op. cit.,* pp. 15–16.

29. An artifact testifying to this was the announced topic of a university seminar in social psychology, "Social Stress in Wild Rabbits." How might the speaker delineate "stress" from "ease," and is it a white bourgeois criterion that separates wild from domesticated rabbits?

30. Robert Frost, "The White-Tailed Hornet."

31. Knight, *loc. cit.,* pp. 331, 336–337.

32. See Matson, *op. cit.,* Chs. VI ff.; Werkmeister, in Gross (ed.), *op. cit.,* p. 490; Eliseo Vivas, "Science and the Studies of Man," in Schoeck and Wiggins (eds.), *op. cit.,* p. 51.

33. This development in the philosophy of science both reflected and fostered the same development in the philosophy of history in the West in the eighteenth and nineteenth centuries, when the progress view gradually supplanted the Christian eschatological view as the established premise. See J. B. Bury, *The Idea of Progress* (London: Macmillan & Co., Ltd., 1920); Frederick J. Teggart (ed.), *The Idea of Progress: A Collection of Readings* (University of California Press, 1949).

34. Howard Hopkins, *The Rise of the Social Gospel in American Protestantism* (Yale University Press, 1940); H. Richard Niebuhr, *The Kingdom of God in America.*

35. Stein, *op. cit.,* to which we will give more attention later. Many other titles sound equally Spenglerian as literature of lament: Karl Mannheim, *Diagnosis of Our Time* (London: Kegan Paul, Trench, Trubner, & Co., 1943); Sorokin, *op. cit.;* Jacques Ellul, *The Technological Society* (Alfred A. Knopf, Inc., 1964); Esther Milner, *The Failure of Success* (Exposition Press, Inc., 1959); C. Wright Mills, *Causes of World War III* (Simon and Schuster, Inc., 1958); Matson, *op. cit.* Many European works might be cited which share a complete disavowal of the progress view.

36. An interesting correction to the rural nostalgia of the urban sociologist might be to analyze the style of life in the "good old days." A look, for example, at Sumner C. Powell, *Puritan Village: The Formation of a New England Town* (Wesleyan University Press, 1963) and its court cases would reveal the corruption and meanness of life among this community of saints.

37. Albert Wissen, "Sociology," in Harold Ditmanson (ed.), *Christian Faith and the Liberal Arts* (Augsburg Publishing House, 1960), p. 229.

38. Mills, *The Sociological Imagination,* p. 67.

39. Werkmeister, in Gross (ed.), *op. cit.,* p. 504. Natanson's Introduction (*op. cit.*) bespeaks the necessity of philosophy in social science thus: "In the study of sociology or economics or political science it is ultimately the universal horizon of these fields which gives them a meaningful placement in the hierarchy of all knowledge. The student who fails to keep constantly before him the transcendent implications of his concrete problems lacks a perspective vital to his life as well as to his work" (p. 26).

40. A few representative titles are W. R. Sorley, *Moral Values and the Idea of God* (London: Cambridge University Press, 1935); George Thomas, *Christian Ethics and Moral Philosophy* (Charles Scribner's Sons, 1955), Ch. 20; Étienne Gilson, *Moral Values and the Moral Life,* tr. by L. R. Ward

(London: B. Herder Book Company, 1931); Ian Ramsey (ed.), *Christian Ethics and Contemporary Problems* (London: SCM Press, Ltd., 1966), approaching the issue from the standpoint of linguistic analysis.

41. The major figures of R. B. Perry, Nicolai von Hartmann, Morris Schlick, G. E. Moore, John Dewey, W. M. Urban, and others have been involved in this polemic.

42. H. Richard Niebuhr, "The Center of Value," first printed in Ruth Anshen (ed.), *Moral Principles of Action* (Harper & Brothers, 1952), and reprinted in H. Richard Niebuhr, *Radical Monotheism and Western Culture.* See George Schrader, "Value and Valuation," in Paul Ramsey (ed.), *Faith and Ethics: The Theology of H. Richard Niebuhr,* for a critical assessment of Niebuhr's view.

43. H. Richard Niebuhr, *Radical Monotheism,* p. 107.

44. *Ibid.,* p. 103.

45. *Ibid.,* p. 112.

V

The Loss of Community in American Society

Now that some of the issues of methodology in ethics and social science have been aired at least, if not settled, our dialogue may turn to matters of moral substance. It will need to be taken for granted, from here on, that the descriptions of American society we deal with are value-charged, that in the assessments of the American style of life are hidden and revealed all sorts of normative points of view, or to use theological language, faith standpoints. Our overall task is to measure and compare these from the standpoint of the Christian faith about man and community.

The middle decades of the twentieth century have seen a large preoccupation of Americans with self-study. No longer a young nation, expending its energy and striding westward to conquer a continent, America has now come of age, with the leisure and the intellectual equipment to turn in on itself and measure its health. There is a vast literature of self-examination. Scholars seem to take a morbid delight in inventories and reflections on every aspect of American life, sexual, recreational, economic, political, racial, religious—all with an eye to picturing the distinctive American genius or style of life. This intense self-consciousness may reflect a failure of nerve on the part of a middle-aged nation, a lurking suspicion about the moral quality of the culture Americans have been so busy building. It may have more positive and idealistic roots. However prompted, the passion to discover its soul or identity seems to be America's main intellectual preoccupation.

It would be difficult even to catalog all the available studies of American values.[1] The data of evidence would range all the way from the photogenic chaos of a copy of *Life* to gloomy Teutonic tomes on the decline of the West. A sampling of several standard works gives evidence of the persistence of certain dominant value preferences that appear to be distinctively American. There is a high degree of consensus amid the variety of listings. A typical one:

1. Effort and optimism
   a. Moral purpose
   b. Rationalism
2. Romantic individualism
   a. Cult of the average man
   b. Tendency to personalize
3. Change a value in itself
4. Pleasure principle
5. Externalism
6. Simple answers
7. Humor
8. Generosity[2]

Robin Williams in *American Society* finds these to be the dominant values: achievement and success, activity and work, a moral orientation, humanitarian mores, efficiency and practicality, belief in progress, material comfort, equality, freedom, external conformity, science and secular rationality, patriotism, "democratic values": in particular, the value of individual personality.[3] William Whyte centers on "scientism, belongingness, and togetherness" as the ruling values in the social ethic of organization man.[4] Abraham Kaplan finds American ethics constituted by certain distinctive readings of the values of liberty, equality, and fraternity.[5]

From these and comparable studies one might glean a master list of values and debate then which might be primary and which derived. But this is hardly a fruitful way of proceeding. Of much more importance, for our dialogue, is what lies behind the esteem given to these goods, and how they stand in relation to each other. What is the meaning of the syndrome of values Americans prize?

Commonly noted in such studies is that these values more

often stand in collision with each other than in neat fit. The high value attached to individual success does not go well with the value of equality or humanitarian generosity.[6] Other contradictions appear, e.g., equality of status vs. prestige of economic class, simplicity and sincerity vs. extravagance and show,[7] security vs. risk. For the large part, of course, Americans are on the surface unaware of these value collisions, however troubled they may be within.

Underneath the unrest about the collisions of value one may detect a shared suspicion about the spiritual condition of the American. In contrast to the spirit of the late nineteenth and early twentieth centuries, with its confidence in man and optimism about history, the twentieth-century studies of the American's life finds him much less self-assured. His spiritual condition is pictured as dismal and his society "sick." The image of man as hero, free and valiant, mastering his environment through energy, courage, piety, and Yankee ingenuity is supplanted by the image of man as victim of ominous impersonal forces over which he has no control. Though the language of the business and advertising world still casts man in the heroic mold, as we have earlier noted, this is interpreted by the social analysts more as idealized rhetoric than real. The image of Horatio Alger or Daniel Boone is much less apt than the pathetic and haunted man of the cartoons of William Steig or James Thurber.

A common mood of these studies of American life, urbanized and industrialized, is a sense of loss, of bewilderment, of moral confusion. In the stead of the positive terms of eighteenth- and nineteenth-century language—progress, growth, hope, character, vision—the semantics of twentieth-century man is negative: crisis, dilemma, loss, predicament, anxiety, dread, fear—these are the key title terms. It is the "Age of Anxiety," rather than of hope. This distemper appears in the areas of an economy of abundance, among people of plenty, where according to the American dream one would expect to hear only the idylls of happiness. Instead, one hears of "a suburban sadness," or dislocation, an "aimlessness, a low-keyed unpleasure."[8] It is not normally a savage or bitter despair. It is rather a quiet desperation, a gentle disillusionment, a cautious despair, a sense of lost purpose, in the mood of Matthew Arnold's *Dover Beach:*

> as on a darkling plain
> Swept with confused alarms of struggle and flight,
> Where ignorant armies clash by night.

When wanton violence breaks out, and public leaders are assassinated, there is a shudder of horror and dread in the American soul, a profound self-doubt and despair. Any measure of the balance of anxiety and hope, of dread and confidence, in the soul of the American is an impression that no questionnaire or sociometrics computer could quantify. Yet the very frequency with which the dark terms recur in the literature of American self-scrutiny is testimony that they speak correctly of the human condition.

An American Paradise Lost

When one asks for a common principle of explanation for the confusion and collision in values in the anatomy of American melancholy, and the widespread failure of nerve, one theme that recurs is the loss of community, as the result of the conditions of an industrialized, urbanized, technological society, and the desperate attempt to find community again.

This spiritual condition is phrased in many different ways: "the dissolution of community,"[9] the "eclipse of community,"[10] the "loss of community,"[11] the condition of "men astray."[12] It is implicit in the acknowledged shift that has taken place from *"Gemeinschaft"* to *"Gesellschaft,"*[13] that is, from the internal relations of common allegiance and trust implied in the word "community" to the external relations or contacts implied in the word "society." The same shift is described in the distinction between "symbiotic" community, as physical proximity and interdependence, and "moral" community, based on shared loyalties and symbols. Arthur Naftalin[14] finds that city life has a high degree of symbiotic community but a very weak sense of moral community. Robert Nisbet defines "community" in the sense of

Gemeinschaft: "The word . . . encompasses all forms of relationship which are characterized by a high degree of personal intimacy, emotional depth, moral commitment, social cohesion, and continuity in time."[15] Robin Williams, likewise, defining moral community in terms of an "integrated" society, finds widespread disintegration in the lack of shared goals and values.[16] In short, "the lonely crowd," or "man alone."

Our present analysis of this *motif* of the loss of community is made explicitly from the point of view of the Christian faith. The thesis to be defended in this chapter and the next is twofold:

1. In the *de*scription of the quality of American life as a loss of community, the implicit moral judgments about *good* community are essentially Christian ones. In other words, when one explores with the social scientist the goodness of the paradise modern man has lost, or from which he has strayed, it turns out to be strikingly similar to the Christian community.

2. Insofar as these studies are *pre*scriptive, offering a way out of the dilemmas of demoralized man, salvation from mass tyranny, the moral norm is that of an individualism which, from the viewpoint of Christian ethics, compounds rather than solves the inherent problem and misses the wisdom of a Christian prescription transcending a simple alternative between individual autonomy and crowd tyranny.

The key terms in Christian thought about man and community come from a theocentric world view. They are all vertical in their referents, finding their sense out of the relations of man to God. The key terms in secular sociological thought are likewise relational, but the transcendent, theological object of reference is now cut off by adherence to what Tillich calls the "principle of immanence."[17] The meaning of man's life is limited to his horizontal or societal relations. The key terms are, so to speak, "rewired" from the original vertical man-to-God "posts" from which they first took their meaning, to horizontal man-to-society posts. Society replaces God as ultimate referent for the relational terms of community. A sociocentric world view supplants a theocentric one. Man is limited to a flat universe, and to kinship only with his fellows. This major switch of relations makes a profound difference in the resulting conceptions of the soul of man and the moral terms of community, sharply put by Daniel Lerner:

> In this new conception [of social science] a man's inner self is no longer fixed and immutable—and indeed inscrutable. The inner self is nowadays no *territoire sacré,* no bondage of terror between a man and his God, but rather a supple relationship between him and his fellows. . . . Under this more generous modern conception of normalcy, deviant personality is not treated as diabolical impiety toward God, but rather as a failure of communication with one's fellow man—a malfunction of the inner mechanism. This is not a curse but an illness, hence it can be cured.[18]

The Nature of Man

There is no need to rehearse the familiar themes of Christian anthropology: man as creature of God, finding his essential relation in a divine source, and given the terms of selfhood in community by his Creator.[19] In the Christian view of man is a strong voluntarism. A man is as he loves. Voluntarism presumes some kind of freedom; existence in the original order of creation is not involuntary, but choices are willed from an acting center of decision. Man is distinct from animal precisely by reason of his capacity to act deliberately toward consciously conceived ends, rather than as driven compulsively by instincts. But his freedom is not the freedom of radical autonomy; it is set within the limits of the order of creation. The terms of his self-realization are set by the Lord of creation; man is subject to the consequences of his own free choice, for good or ill, for heaven or hell. So consequential freedom in the Christian view is conjoined with a divine determinism in such a dialectical way as that neither pole cancels the other out.

Are there any parallels in sociological theory for this Christian order of creation? At first sight, no. For what chiefly impresses the cultural anthropologist is the vast range of plural cultures. He is suspicious of all fixed and universal generalizations about man, since all he can see are particular societies and particular men. Yet on second and closer look, there can be detected behind the obvious relativities and pluralism certain common "given" elements that are universal. When the sociologist speaks of these qualities shared by man in primitive or modern societies, Aztec or Caltech, living on the island of Manhattan or Fiji, he is pointing to what the Christian theologian means by the "order of creation." Robert Lynd affirms, for instance, that all men in whatever cultures display universal "cravings," such as for "the sense of growth, of realization of personal powers," or for "a physical and psychological security," or for "the expression of his capacities through rivalry and competition, with resulting recognition of status," or for "human mutuality, the sharing of purposes, feelings, and action with others," or for "coherence in the direction and meaning of the behavior to which it entrusts itself."[20] It is significant that such cultural anthropologists as George Murdoch, Margaret Mead, and Ralph Linton detect certain universal qualities or "dominant values" in the most widely disparate cultures.[21]

In these studies, it may indeed be understood that man is a creature of culture, rather than of God, genetically speaking, that these universal cravings and loves arise in a societal matrix, but there is a sense also in which these are understood as ontologically *prior* to culture, that cultural institutions body forth the given demands and innate qualities of human nature.

In the sociological assumptions about human nature one may note also the striking parallel between Christian voluntarism and such judgments as that man is an "affiliative" being, a "belonging" creature, with a built-in "directional orientation,"[22] whose inner character is like that toward which his will is aimed. Riesman's character typology is based on this kind of voluntarism. Likewise this voluntarism presumes human freedom. Though by the canons of its task as a descriptive science sociology is inevitably deterministic, picturing a man's behavior as caused by this or that factor, driven by the car he drives, crushed by the crowd, it is not a simple, one-way determinism. There is also the note of freedom-within-determinism, the assumption that by taking thought man may alter the character of his cities, may free the human spirit, may learn to cope with the bewildering complex of his vast urban sprawl, may recall and relive the terms of community he has lost. Such a presumption, which undergirds the diagnosis of the "sick society" and the proposals for recovery of its health, makes no sense apart from a faith, shared by the Christian, that man is genuinely a free creature, though not simply or purely free. He finds his authentic freedom by coming to right terms with ultimate reality—whether that be conceived as Society or as a Reality transcending society.

Vocation and Identity

A key Christian term in the concept of community is *vocation*. In the order of creation, a self finds his unique individuality by being called by God from out of the people and given a distinctive name. The Biblical concept of vocation is a relational term, with vertical and horizontal referents. The self is called by God and also then sent by God for a special task to meet a moral need of the people of God.

In contemporary sociological theory, the concept of "identity" is of course a master theme.[23] It is the secular analogue for the Christian term "vocation," now reoriented to the ultimate reality of Society. It is not vis-à-vis God, but vis-à-vis Society that one is to discover or recover one's self-awareness. As a psychological category "identity" connotes integrity, a sense of oneness and constancy, in contrast to scattered disintegration. This parallels "faithfulness" in Christian discourse. In modern social theory, heavily infused with Freudian categories, the search for identity is carried on in the traffic of encounter of the self with the shifting crowds. A man engages in role-playing, now identifying with this group, now with that, now putting on this image and now that, in order to find who he really is. He does not look within but without, to the crowd, for his nature.

All this is significant as equivalent to the Christian doctrine of man in the original order of creation. For much of the literature of identity presumes that there is some kind of integrity of selfhood that is "there," or "given," although now lost or obscured, and that the task is not so much to create one's identity as to recover or recall it.

The Fall of Man, in Theology and Sociology

Any self-respecting sociologist who feels himself emancipated from a Christian world view and whatever casual Sunday school nurture he might have had as a youth would hardly find relevant to his investigation of culture the classical terms of Protestant theology. The Adamic fall, original sin, and pride seem to him quaint relics from an apparatus of thought that appears shabbily out of place in the halls of science. Even the brilliant efforts of a Reinhold Niebuhr to restore the relevance of certain classic Christian terms[24] have not reestablished them as common currency among journeymen sociologists. Yet if one reviews the original meaning of these Christian words and frees them of the mechanical Biblical literalism in which they are commonly mistaken, points of striking parallel and contrast between the Christian and sociologist's picture of the human condition come into view.

For the Christian view of man in history, the symbol of the fall of man points to the recurring phenomenon of man's rebellion in "pride" against his Creator and his attempt to substitute his own self as sovereign. Pride's primary relation is vertical: it means revolt, in the first instance, against God, and idolatry of self. But there are social consequences and implications. Pride results in alienation and estrangement from neighbor and nature. The original community of creation, wherein man lives in faithful obedience to God's law of love, and in right relation to his neighbor, is broken from man's side through the misuse of his created freedom.

Anomie and the Loss of Community

Our epoch's providence is quite worn out,
The Lion of nothing chases us about.
(W. H. Auden.)

In the many sociological analyses of the spiritual malaise of man in contemporary society, one does not encounter any key term analogous to "pride" (or *hubris*) as the root explanation of man's loss of community. But one does meet two dominant themes which provide intriguing points of parallel: *anomie* and *alienation.* These terms permeate the literature of cultural diagnosis in the twentieth century, much as the terms "progress" and "freedom" permeated the thought of the nineteenth. Both terms are relational, as well as negative inversions of something positive. *Anomie,* or normlessness, presumes some normal order lost. Alienation, or estrangement, presumes some original right relationship that has been broken. To grasp the meaning of what it is to be anomic, or alienated, then, one must presume some kind of ontology, some kind of "given" order of norms, or community of persons, remembered even in the absence of them, just as to know a lie for a lie implies a recollection of an order of truth, or to recognize rationalization implies affirmation of the true reasoning which it falsifies. So too these negative terms carry the memory and echo of an original right law and true community.

The term *anomie,* started in circulation by the sociologist Émile Durkheim, has taken on many turns and shades of meaning, a richness that the simple word "normlessness" does not quite convey.[25]

In the first place, it is an inner, voluntaristic term, referring to a kind of condition of the soul in its valuations. It is not mere pluralism of values,[26] or heterogeneity in the loves from which plural actions spring. It is something more than the collision of values in the soul of the body politic, where cooperation and competition, or tolerance and sternness, may vex each other, though a bewilderment in the face of incompatible values is a clear symptom of *anomie.*[27] It is rather more a lack of the principle of order or moral authority whereby to make moral choices and to adjudicate among colliding values. It is a dislocation or disintegration in the fundamental loyalties of the self, who has no supreme court of moral appeal, or an ultimate authority shared in common with his neighbors, or "a state of de-regulation in which social norms . . . do not control men's actions."[28] In briefest terms, it is a loss of the understanding of the binding terms of community. There is no King in Israel, and "every man does what is righteous in his own sight."

Talcott Parsons defines it thus:

> *Anomie* may perhaps most briefly be characterized as the state where large numbers of individuals are to a serious degree lacking in the kind of integration with stable institutional patterns which is essential to their own personal stability and to the smooth functioning of the social system.[29]

Robert Merton defines it as "a breakdown in cultural structure, when there is an acute disjunction between cultural norms and the socially structured capacities of the members of the group to act in accord with them."[30]

Robert MacIver more loosely describes it as "the state of mind of one who has been pulled up from his moral roots, who has no longer any standards but only disconnected urges, who has no longer any sense of continuity, of folk, of obligation . . . spiritually sterile, responsive only to himself, responsible to no one."[31]

It would be quite too complex a problem to trace out the historical and ideological roots of *anomie*. One could plausibly account for it as the spiritual aftermath of the external processes of industrialization and urbanization that sever the ties of man with traditional authorities and uproot him from the securities of soil and stabilities of kinfolk.[32] Or one may as plausibly explain the source of *anomie* by the inner disintegration of the mind of Western man, starting with the Renaissance, which produces then the disintegration of his cultural institutions, from politics to art, becoming the outer expression of his inner anarchy.[33] In the last analysis, the lines of causation should be drawn both ways, from soul to institutions, from institutions to soul.[34]

Anomie also means anarchy, or a normless freedom. In the various discussions of the prevalence of *anomie* in modern life, the term has a pejorative ring, a gray aspect. It is significant that the term "freedom," celebrated joyfully in the nineteenth century as the great good, now rings in the twentieth with a more doleful sound. The revolt from tradition and authority which seemed such a clear good to nineteenth-century man results in this century in the dizziness of freedom. The existentialists speak of man as "imprisoned in freedom" (Sartre). Existential freedom has been called the French flu. "Nausea" is a word common among the Sartreans. A normless anarchy produces a new kind of tyranny, a paralysis of action.

There is still another characteristic of an anomic or faithless generation frequently remarked in studies of American society: the attempt to escape from the dizziness of freedom by a fierce and total allegiance to authority. A condition of complete *anomie,* one may say, is intolerable; it violates a demand in human nature as strong as the need for freedom: the need to belong. If *anomie* represents the loss of traditional authorities and norms, it produces a kind of vacuum into which rush new authorities, new messiahs. "The king is dead! Long live the king!"

This thesis makes considerable sense when tested against the data of mass behavior in politics and religion. To escape from freedom, men revert to authority. To overcome a sense of cosmic loneliness and rootlessness, they rush to this or that instant community.[35] The call to rebel from a dead tradition is less compelling for modern anomic man than the call to believe and belong.[36]

In American religious life, this reversion to authority appears in the widespread appeal of evangelical revivalism and Biblical Fundamentalism. Do not question; do not doubt. Simply believe. Come to Christ. The Bible says. . . . The simplistic answers given, the charismatic appeal of vivid personal leadership in the evangelist, and the black-and-white authority of the Bible, are ready devices whereby men are promised the recovery of their lost identity and the terms of true community with God.

Politically, instant community is provided in the totalitarian mind-set, whether that be in the form of national socialism or the Americanism of the American Legion or the John Birch Society. Racially, the same phenomenon appears in the tribal loyalty engendered in the K.K.K., the White Citizens Councils, the Black Muslims, or in one or another Black Power organizations. *Anomie* is overcome by identification with those of like color, through intense consciousness of kind in warfare against "the others." More vaguely, perhaps, yet more pervasively, the passion for conformity, so widely noted in the ethics of the American suburbanite, may find its most plausible explanation as the attempt to escape *anomie* by belonging to the middle-class tribe, finding one's identity by losing it in meticulous imitation of its tribal standards and ceremonial rites.

To interpret this condition of *anomie* from a Christian perspective, it is evident that there are striking points of contrast as there are striking points of similarity. Where the classic Christian view of sin puts it as "pride," an active rebellion and defiance of God's rule in aggressive self-centeredness, the sociologist's conception is rather more of a condition of sickness that brings man low through no fault of his own. It is no accident that the phrase in vogue is "sick society," not "sinful society." Man is the passive victim of the malaise of *anomie*. Who or what is responsible for his fall? The answer is as elusive as it is in the myth of Genesis: Is it Adam, or Eve, or the serpent? Broadly speaking, the explanation of the source of the trouble is in terms of the vast collective processes and systems over which the individual man has little control. What has "eclipsed" community in contemporary America and lost for man the true terms of fraternity? The city, the machine, the bureaucracy, answers Maurice Stein,[37] summarizing the views of many other sociologists. These are the "world-rulers of this present darkness." But they are not taken, as with Paul, for cosmic powers. The demons are man-made, prowling in the economic and political institutions. Again, it can readily be seen how the key term of "sin"—if it can be called that—is "rewired" from theistic to societal posts, and the derived meaning is thereby radically changed.

At the same time, there remains a striking point of similarity. We have seen how anomic man, uprooted from the traditional roots and stays and norms of community, dizzy in his freedom and aimless in his direction, attempts to escape his freedom through identification with one or another parochial group, in surrender to authority, in fierce belonging. This phenomenon, so readily confirmed by empirical evidence, may be taken as confirmation of the Christian view of man: that he is a "normful" creature, created to belong to something or someone outside himself, in devotion to whom he finds meaning in his existence. To put it yet another way, he is a religious being, a subject demanding an "object of ultimate concern," a transcendent authority. The ethical question then is transformed. It is not: Should man be free, or should he belong? It is rather: How true are the objects of his inevitable belonging? How valid are his gods? Who in his pantheon sets the terms of authentic community? Which are the saving gods and which are idols with feet of clay? In the service of what god is perfect freedom found? What gods are the tyrants? The Christian interpreter of these signs of the times will be able to detect, within the mass movements of organized man and his intense tribal loyalties, the echoes of Augustine's famous prayer: "Thou hast created us for Thyself, and our spirits are restless until they come to rest in Thee."

Alienation

Alienation is a term even more frequently encountered in the literature of cultural lament than *anomie*. They are correlate concepts. Both are relational; both are in the minor key. Alienation, coming into the currency of twentieth-century sociological discourse from many sources, is variously and imprecisely used, and it eludes the quantitative measurement that sociometrics might like to give it. Yet it remains, like *anomie,* an apt empirical generalization for the shared experience of lost community.[38]

As a relational, subject-object term, the meaning of alienation depends greatly on the referent: *From* what or whom is the self estranged? Where was man's home, whence as prodigal he has wandered? The original referent for the term, of course, was theological: the first estrangement in the garden was from God. According to Feuer, Calvin is the first to use the term explicitly,[39] but actually it goes much farther back and is implicit or explicit in Luther, Augustine, and the mythology of Genesis. Man's estrangement from God is the root of his alienation from his neighbor beside him and nature below him. In contemporary social thought, so deeply influenced by Marx and the Freudians, the term has been secularized, "rewired" to mean a disorientation from society or nature. In Marxian thought man is alienated from the work of his hands by the machine and from his neighbor by the power structures of capitalism. The conditions of industrial work in the city uproot him from his native soil and crowd him into the city, where he drifts, a nomad with no hearth or home.[40] And finally, as his condition is further interpreted by the Freudians, man is alienated from himself, schizophrenic to greater or less degree, harassed by inner demons of his own making, the neurotic personality.

In these secular translations of the theological meaning of alienation, it is significant to note that the experience is something more tragic and ominous than the subject's simply being at a distance from its prized object. Not only is the alienated self away from its referent, it is "over-against" its referent. It is more, then, than a *loss* of community. It is the contention, the warfare of the self with his origins, the collision of the parts within the universal whole.

The chief preoccupation of social science, as it interprets America's spiritual condition, has been with the horizontal dimension: man and the crowd.[41] With many variations, the theme is heard of man's ambivalent relation to the collective: his estrangement *from* true community through the conspiracy of social forces, turning the crowd into enemy, the threat to his identity, yet withal man's turning *to* the crowd as savior, to overcome his alienation. The crowd is treated as both enemy and friend, demon and savior.

Anonymity and Chromium Community

As earlier noted, alienation is not a simple term. There are cognate meanings that cluster around it, all negative: "powerlessness, meaninglessness, normlessness, isolation, and self-estrangement," according to one interpreter.[42] Another term close by is anonymity, the experience of depersonalization. This is perhaps the most dismal aspect of urban man's experience of himself, as the consequence of the mechanization of his work life, and the depersonalization of his organization. The machine turns him from person into thing, a "hand," an economic unit capable of just so much output in his work. And in social relations, the "organization" comes in between man and man, between the "I" and the "Thou," vitiating the relationship of authentic community in deep personal trusts and common loyalties into impersonal contacts of "its" that have to deal with each other shrewdly and calculatingly as things, commodities, customers, cases.

Looked at through the eyes of the Christian faith, it is a sign of the order of creation persisting in the order of corruption that in this vast sea of impersonality and anonymity, men search for islands of community. To be human one must have a face and a name. So men carry on their business and political relationships in highly "personalized" form. "Folksiness" in campaigning is cultivated as a political strategy: a Rockefeller makes his way with the proletariat campaigning on the street corners with the greeting: "Hi, fellah." In the giant corporation, there is a carefully contrived attempt to overcome anonymity by "personalizing" all contacts: personalized memos, personalized name tags, personalized checkbooks, and friendly first-name Rotarian gambits used in the competitive struggle.[43] The successful operator is he who hails the largest number of people by their first names. In sales transaction in the big store, the personal language of Christian community is heavily used: "May I help you?" "A & P cares." "We are here to serve you." All parties understand, of course, that the real motives behind the phrases are considerably less disinterested and benevolent than they sound.

An amusing artifact marking the attempt to overcome anonymity and alienation by pseudo-personalized devices is the spiel of the airline stewardess, read from a card over the intercom to the anonymous blobs of humanity, all utter strangers, huddled together over an abyss of 20,000 feet. "Captain Smythe is in command. Miss Daugherty and Miss Sutherland are your stewardesses. We would like to express our real pleasure at having you aboard. If there is anything we can do to make your trip more enjoyable, do let us know. . . . We sincerely hope you'll join us again soon." This folksy ritual of reassurance is supposed to unite all the strangers into one intimate family of warmth and trust, mothered by the stewardess. Yet even her individualized farewells to the passengers as they leave ("By-by"—"By now") are marks of mechanical community, a chromium coziness and plastic fellowship.

From what standpoint may one interpret this airline ritual as amusing if not pathetic, and recognize the phony quality of the friendliness of commercial relation? Whence this lurking suspicion of the self that he is being "taken in" by the gambits of apparent generosity, and manipulated into buying something? What other than a memory, dimly recalled, of authentic community, an order of mutual openness and unguarded personal trust, once lived in the order of creation?

Conformity

We need to attend to a final quality commonly noted in the studies of mass culture: *conformity*. This of course is a favorite theme of the novels and plays whose heroes (or victims) contend against the dark forces in the mass media and the establishment that conspire to break their spirit. They fight the system for a while but usually fail. The organization man in the gray flannel suit plays it safe. His itch of egoism is drowned in the lotions of the system. The conformist is the subject of a similar scrutiny in the well-known studies already used herein of David Riesman, William Whyte, Erich Fromm, C. Wright Mills, and many others.[44]

For the purposes of our study on community, the phenomenon of conformity is to be seen as an expression of man's attempt to escape his freedom by compulsive belonging, by imitation, by hiding in the collective. The passion for keeping up with the style in dress, from hairdos to toe shape, is more than an idiosyncracy of adolescent girls. It covers America like a smog. The denizens of suburbia drive standardized cars to and from standardized houses in standardized developments, exchanging with each other (as though fresh discoveries) the standardized opinions derived from the syndicated newspaper columns and the TV commentator. Yet at the same time, the victim must be nurtured in the illusion that he is distinctive. The new dress must deviate slightly from the uniform. (Advertising plays strange tricks with regimentation and independence to secure conformity: "Smoke Viceroy, the cigarette of the man who thinks for himself." "The Dodge Rebellion wants you.")

As man cannot live by bread alone, being created a spiritual being, he demands some sense of significance in his existence, else he will commit suicide. If he be alienated in the ways we have described from the traditional bonds of community, he will fashion for himself new bonds and substitute new sources of meaning. He cannot stand sheer insignificance. So he bridges over the chasm of alienation by devices of every sort, to establish the work of his hands and the loves of his heart, to fix their meaning to last against time's flood and as stay against utter despair.

The compulsion to conform may be translated into religious terms as man's total response of will to his condition of alienation by attempted reconciliation with the god of his life, the crowd. This reconciliation can be effected, and community restored, he is persuaded, by his finding acceptance and forgiveness at the hands of his peers, the anonymous authorities in the crowd, as Erich Fromm describes them,[45] who decree the proper ways of salvation. "Alienation" and "reconciliation," the Christian terms of the drama of redemption, are now repeated in an immanental form. Mass man believes ardently in the doctrine of justification by the grace of the crowd. His careful ethics of conformity may be interpreted both as signs of his acceptance and as his efforts to earn it. Plainly, this is again a primal reorientation in a doctrine of salvation, from the vertical point of reference to the horizontal. It is not the Lord God but the crowd whom we meet in the final analysis, the secular Last Judgment.

Whatever be the official words of his prayers in church, the real prayer in the heart of the believer might be phrased thus: "May the words of my mouth, and the meditations of my heart, be acceptable in thy sight, O Crowd, my strength and my redeemer."

This fundamental shift of primal orientation has a profound effect on the morality or "value system" of the American. A few of these may be noted. While the moral terms take their origin from a Christian world view, they now stand for something very different from their first meaning.

Take the word "equality," for example. In its classic Christian form, it meant a common creatureliness, containing the infinite richness of plural differences. Now, though voiced in the rhetoric of "the worth and dignity of the individual," when mass man says "all men are equal" he really means "all men are the same, or alike." It is a leveling concept. When applied to political affairs, this leads to a doctrine of conformity to the homogenized democratic mass,[46] suspicious of deviant behavior, tolerant of the contrary mind only as long as he does not disturb the Establishment.

Another term that has undergone a profound sea change in this secularization of world views has been the simple word "love." As we have earlier reviewed it, the original Christian meaning derived from the theocentric referent. Out of a heart of gratitude, the Christian was to seek the neighbor's good as the fulfillment of theocentric obligation. Now, in the flat world of crowds, love's credentials are entirely secularized. Its validity is pragmatic or utilitarian. Deeds of concern and service are good because they prove successful devices of group adjustment, instruments of conformity. So love is a kind of lubricant in the parts of the social machinery. Thus the "social ethics" of friendliness and fellowship has replaced the "Protestant Ethic," according to William Whyte,[47] and the "glad hand" replaced the "unseen hand," according to David Riesman.[48] The *agape* of I Corinthians, chapter 13, which "suffereth long, . . . is kind, . . . is not puffed up, . . . is not easily provoked," becomes the great tranquilizer prescribed by the Organization that soothes like

Muzak all irritants and assures amicable concord of like with like, in smooth functioning. The great commandment becomes: "Be sociable. Have a Pepsi."

From Station to Status

In the godly community of Puritan times, the sense of worth and dignity of each person derived from his *station* before God, and his calling by God for a special vocation of service in the divine economy. In Parkwood Forest, the suburban community of organization man, the sense of worth and meaning for its members comes from the prestige in the *status* each enjoys in the eyes of his neighbors. The so-called game of status-seeking by the competitive acquisition of status symbols is more than a game. It is a deadly serious business, a "religious" matter, for one's life depends on being accepted, or justified by the crowd, or whoever in the crowd are its high priests of taste. But the crowd can see only the exterior. Man is accepted, then, in terms of how he looks, by his seeming, not his inner being. So one may account for the externals, the preoccupation with creating an image, with appearances, with role-playing, to the total neglect of internal integrity, the secret self, since there is no One who sees and rewards in secret. In what C. Wright Mills calls "the status-panic," one may detect a profound conversion in the dominant moral values, from the Puritan era to the suburban era of the present, epitomized in the shift from station to status.[49] In the Puritan age, at least ideally speaking, a man was to *do* good in whatever station God had called him, out of responsible love to the God revealed in Christ. In the Yankee era, a man was to *make* good, and move up by pluck and luck to a position of eminence on the social ladder. God was fading from the Yankee's sight as the One to whom man is accountable. In the contemporary age, the ideal of the organization man, the operator, is to *look* good, since the Crowd is the reality to whom alone he feels accountable.[50] From doing good, to making good, to looking good: this is the profound ethical changeover in the American's style of life and in the real theology that guides his life.

To all these analyses of *anomie,* alienation, anonymity, and conformity, whatever their cultural roots and sources, there clings a certain bad aroma. The descriptions are not value-free, but treated as disvalues, as connoting something precious lost in human relations. The phrase "mass manipulation," for example, is a pejorative term: it is a wrong committed against human dignity that man is exploited by the engineering of propaganda. Conformity is likewise a pejorative term: there is something that violates what human relations ought to be, something tragic in man's attempt to overcome alienation by resignation to the crowd. It is pathetic that man is nameless, "thingified." There is something phony in the status sought by the status seekers, that they sense even as they seek it. The crucial ethical question then to ask is: From what perch transcendent of the crowd is one able to make this negative evaluation? Why does the ethics of conformity fail to yield the identity and authentic existence it promises? For a thoroughgoing answer to these troublesome questions we come back to our original thesis: that the value judgments between the lines of the negative analysis of the lonely crowd are made from the standpoint of the Christian norms of community, whether the indebtedness be unconscious or acknowledged. It is something like Christian community, in short, that has been lost in American society. It is its haunting memory that prompts the note of lament in the self-analysis.

What, then, shall we do to be saved, to recover community, if indeed any promises can be held out? For a critical comparison of the ways out—or the ways back—prescribed by social analyst and Christian theologian, we turn to the next chapter.

NOTES

1. Clyde Kluckhohn lists eight pages of bibliography at the close of his essay "Have There Been Discernible Shifts in Values During the Past Generation?" in E. E. Morison (ed.), *The American Style* (Harper & Brothers, 1958), pp. 207–214, hereafter cited as "Shifts in Values," and this is only a sampling of the literature of two decades.

2. Robin Williams, *American Society,* p. 151. Also Clyde Kluckhohn, "Generalized Orientation and Class Patterns," in Lyman Bryson (ed.), *Conflicts of Power in Modern Culture,* Conference on Science, Philosophy, and Religion in Their Relation to the Democratic Way of Life, Seventh Symposium (Harper & Brothers, 1947).

3. Williams, *op. cit.,* Ch. XI.

4. William H. Whyte, Jr., *The Organization Man* (Simon and Schuster, Inc., 1956), Chs. 3, 4, 5.

5. Abraham Kaplan, "American Ethics and Public Policy," in Morison (ed.), *op. cit.,* pp. 3–107.

6. Tocqueville remarked this contradiction in the American a century and a half ago.

7. Cf. Kluckhohn, "Shifts in Values," pp. 152–155.

8. See the essay of David Riesman, "The Suburban Sadness," in W. M. Dobriner (ed.), *The Suburban Community* (G. P. Putnam's Sons, 1958); reprinted in Philip Olson (ed.), *America as a Mass Society* (The Free Press of Glencoe, Inc., 1963), as "The Suburban Dislocation."

9. Olson (ed.), *op. cit.*

10. Maurice R. Stein, *The Eclipse of Community.*

11. Robert Nisbet, *The Quest for Community,* Ch. I.

12. Robert Angell, *Free Society and Moral Crisis* (University of Michigan Press, 1958), Ch. I.

13. See Ferdinand Tönnies, *Community and Society.* The most complete and discerning treatment of the concept of community in nineteenth-century sociology, based on the distinction in Tönnies between *Gemeinschaft* and *Gesellschaft,* is to be found in Robert Nisbet, *The Sociological Tradition.* The author takes "community" as one of the unit-ideas in classical nineteenth-century social theory and shows its centrality to the thought of Comte, LePlay, Tönnies, Weber, Durkheim, and Simmel.

14. Arthur Naftalin *et al., An Introduction to Social Science: Personality, Work, Community* (J. B. Lippincott Company, 1953), Pt. III, pp. 3–6.

15. Robert Nisbet, *The Sociological Tradition* (Basic Books, Inc., 1966), p. 47.

16. Williams, *op. cit.,* Chs. X, XIV.

17. Paul Tillich, *Theology of Culture* (Oxford University Press, 1959), p. 43.

18. Daniel Lerner, "Social Science, Whence and Whither," in *The Human Meaning of the Social Sciences,* p. 17. This passage also illustrates by its stereotype a naïveté about Christian anthropology and the concept of sin.

19. See Chapter II, above.

20. Robert S. Lynd, *Knowledge for What?,* pp. 191–197.

21. See, for example, Ralph Linton's *Study of Man* (D. Appleton-Century Company, Inc., 1936) or *The Tree of Culture* (Alfred A. Knopf, Inc., 1955); or Margaret Mead, "Cultural Man" in Egbert de Vries (ed.), *Man in Community,* pp. 197–218.

22. Lynd, *op. cit.,* p. 47.

23. See Maurice R. Stein and others, *Identity and Anxiety* (The Free Press of Glencoe, Inc., 1960). See also Allen Wheelis, *The Quest for Identity* (W. W. Norton & Company, Inc., 1958); Erving Goffmann, *The Presentation of Self in Everyday Life* (Edinburgh: University of Edinburgh, Social Research Center, 1956; Doubleday & Company, Inc., 1959).

24. Especially Reinhold Niebuhr's famous Gifford Lectures, *The Nature and Destiny of Man.* The view of human sin in the discussion below presumes the kind of Christian interpretation of sin explicated in his pages.

25. Of the many treatments of *anomie* in sociological literature from Durkheim on, the following may be taken as representative. For Durkheim himself, treatments of the theme appear in *Suicide* and elsewhere. A selection from Durkheim on *anomie* is to be found in C. Wright Mills (ed.), *Images of Man* (George Braziller, Inc., 1960). See Robert Nisbet, *The Sociological Tradition,* pp. 300–304. For a fuller introduction to Durkheim, consult Robert Nisbet (ed.), *Émile Durkheim, with Selected Essays* (Prentice-Hall, Inc., 1965). Karl Mannheim's *Diagnosis of Our Time* (London: Kegan Paul, Trench, Trubner & Co., 1943) treats the phenomenon as "the crisis in valuation." Contemporary treatments of the theme are to be found in Robert Merton, *Social Theory and Social Structure,* Chs. 4 and 5; Esther Milner,

The Failure of Success; Robert M. MacIver, *The Ramparts We Guard* (The Macmillan Company, 1950), Ch. X; Milton Yinger, "On *Anomie,*" *Journal for the Scientific Study of Religion,* Vol. III (April, 1964); Howard Becker, "Normative Reactions to Normlessness," *American Sociological Review,* Vol. 25 (Dec., 1960). Two treatments of *anomie* in political form are Sebastian de Grazia, *The Political Community: A Study in Anomie* (The University of Chicago Press, 1948), and Angell, *op. cit.*

26. Yinger, *loc. cit.,* p. 159.

27. Robin Williams, *op. cit.,* p. 564.

28. Yinger, *loc. cit.,* p. 159.

29. Talcott Parsons, *Essays in Sociological Theory* (The Free Press of Glencoe, Inc., 1954), p. 125.

30. Merton, *op. cit.,* p. 162.

31. MacIver, *op. cit.,* p. 84.

32. Stein, *op. cit.,* seems to follow this line of explanation.

33. Roman Catholic writers such as Christopher Dawson or Gabriel Marcel characteristically interpret the matter this way.

34. This version of the chicken-egg problem is well analyzed in Winston White, *Beyond Conformity* (The Free Press of Glencoe, Inc., 1961), pp. 16–50, where he delineates between the "moralizer" and the "reformer."

35. Eric Hoffer, *The True Believer: Thoughts on the Nature of Mass Movements* (Harper & Brothers, 1951).

36. Nisbet, *The Quest for Community,* p. 26.

37. Stein, *op. cit.* See typically, Hendrik M. Ruitenbeck (ed.), *The Dilemma of Organizational Society* (E. P. Dutton & Company, Inc., 1963).

38. Lewis Feuer, "What Is Alienation? The Career of a Concept," in Stein and Vidich, *op. cit.,* pp. 127–147, is a competent sketch, more valuable than one given in a semisatiric essay of Daniel Bell, "Sociodicy: A Guide to Modern Usage," *The American Scholar,* Vol. 35 (Autumn, 1966), pp. 698–702, in which he traces the transformation in the usage of the term. See Nisbet, *The Sociological Tradition,* Ch. 7; White, *op. cit.,* pp. 44–49.

39. Feuer, *loc. cit.,* p. 128.

40. Whyte, *op. cit.,* Ch. 21, "The Transients."

41. We bypass here the consideration of the complex issues of man's alienation from nature, posed by the industrial revolution and technology. It might be noted, as a working hypothesis, that whereas man has lost his kinship with nature, and it stands over against him as hostile threat, modern man has a high confidence in his powers to overcome his alienation from nature and recover community, through technical manipulation. It is ironic that the same newspaper that carried the account of the docking of a spaceship in outer space, the achievement of technical community with split-second accuracy, also contains the account of the brutal warfare of man with his neighbor in South Vietnam. It is as though man possesses the key to the terms of community with nature but cannot find the key to the terms of community with neighbor. The irony becomes tragic in that man in the mastering of nature may become the instrument of his self-destruction.

42. Melvin Seeman, "On the Meaning of Alienation," *American Sociological Review,* Vol. 24 (Dec., 1959). See F. H. Heinemann, *Existentialism and the Modern Predicament* (London: A. & C. Black, Ltd., 1954).

43. William Whyte's *The Organization Man* is the most thoroughgoing "field study" documenting this generalization available. See also David Riesman, *The Lonely Crowd,* Ch. XIII; Nisbet, *Quest for Community,* p. 30.

44. The most significant books and articles out of the recent prodigious literature on conformity and nonconformity are listed in White, *op. cit.,* pp. 213–225.

45. Erich Fromm, *The Sane Society,* p. 153.

46. Dwight MacDonald, "A Theory of Mass Culture," in Bernard Rosenberg and David Manning White (eds.), *Mass Culture* (The Free Press of Glencoe, Inc., 1957).

47. Whyte, *op. cit.,* Ch. II.

48. Riesman, *The Lonely Crowd,* p. 150.

49. C. Wright Mills, *White Collar* (Oxford University Press, Inc., 1951), p. 239, and Ch. III. For further treatment of the theme of status-seeking, see Riesman's treatment of the "other-directed" character, *The Lonely Crowd,* Ch. VI; Williams, *op. cit.,* p. 462; Kluckhohn, "Shifts in Values," p. 185; de Grazia, *op. cit.,* p. 218; and Whyte, *op. cit.,* p. 399.

50. This shift in the American style of ethics is more fully treated in Waldo Beach, *The Christian Life* (The CLC Press, 1967), Ch. 13, "Christian Vocation in an Industrial Society."

VI

The Recovery of Community: Sociological and Christian Prescriptions

In the previous chapter we have attempted to explicate the ethical value judgments permeating the descriptive analyses of American culture in the mid-twentieth century. Certain moral generalizations stand forth plainly. The conformity of mass culture does violence to something sacred and precious in human nature. Supine resignation to mass engineering of taste is dehumanizing. Behind the benign face of the forces conspiring to manipulate choices and guide Americans to a promised land are vicious intentions. The promises of community prove to be delusions. Man remains isolated and anxious, demoralized by a nameless dread. All these judgments permeating the sociological literature convey the doleful tenor of the times. They are estimates that could not be made except from some vantage point up and away from the crowd, at sufficient distance to be able to see that the ethic of conformity is really leading away from the utopia promised by those in command on the ground.

From a Christian standpoint, it is highly significant that most of the major and minor prophets who have been crying in the American wilderness go beyond jeremiads about the loss of community to offer solutions and paths out of the woods. What shall we do to be saved? Some prescriptions are offered, and some remedies proposed, albeit tentatively and cautiously. This may be a reflection only of the effervescence of the frontier optimism of America. Or it may reflect a deeper unconscious indebtedness to the Christian tradition, in its view of man and his destiny, with its confidence that there is salvation accessible even in the worst times, and that beyond judgment are the promises of grace. In any case, these writers see urban decay in the city of man, but also signs of urban renewal. How valid the remedy may prove to be from a Christian standpoint remains to be seen.

Walden Two: Individualism Revisited

The prescription suggested by many secular physicians is a new autonomy. If conformity to the mass be the devastation of community, then what is needed is a fresh declaration of independence from the crowd in a recovery of authentic individualism.

The saving autonomy proposed is an ideal quite more subtle than the rhetoric of a Republican individualism fighting against "creeping socialism." But it does represent some nostalgia for the nineteenth-century hero. As over against the conformist, resigned or petulant, the escape from collectivism is apparently by way of an individualism no longer "rugged" perhaps, but at least one freed from conformity.

David Riesman calls for a new autonomy.[1] It is a style of life different from that of the "inner-directed" self, to be sure. It is not antisocial but develops organically out of "other-direction,"[2] yet is like the inner-directed self in its power to choose its own goals and pace. (The goals that should be chosen are not indicated.) William Whyte, in his critique of the shortcomings of the established "social ethic" of togetherness, is wisely coy about offering a pat solution. "There is no solution. The conflict between individual and society has always involved dilemma; it always will, and it is intellectual arrogance to think a program would solve it."[3] But the inference of his hints for salvation are prescriptions of nonconformity. Fight the organization from inside.[4] Erich Fromm celebrates the rebirth of creative, productive individuals, who love others as an extension of their self-love.[5] Having identified alienation as the problem of modern society, C. Wright Mills counterposes to "the system" the "free and rational individual" as offering what modest solution is possible.[6]

A recent study of community by Winston White, a disciple of Talcott Parsons, takes exception to the generalization that contemporary urban man has lost his soul in the tyranny of the mass. In the increasing differentiation of function of a technological society White finds a larger scope of freedom, and the occasion at least for wider creativity for the individual. The city offers emancipation for the human spirit, enabling the single individual to move beyond conformity.[7]

No one of these influential thinkers is so romantic or naïve as to propose a physical escape from megapolis in solitary pilgrimage to a rural Walden. The city, the machine, the giant corporation, are here to stay. The claim only is for some individualistic footing, "in but not of the world" of the collective, whereon the self may with some measure of integrity and serenity say "yes" or "no" to the crowd within which he stands. Distant echoes are heard here of Emerson: "It is easy in the world to live after the world's opinion; it is easy in solitude to live after our own; but the great man is he who in the midst of the crowd keeps with perfect sweetness the independence of solitude."[8]

Agape and *Anomie*

How does this prescription look from the standpoint of Christian ethics and the norm of Christian community defined in earlier chapters? This secular salvation is delimited to a one-dimensional immanental universe. It is thin man in a flat world, to be saved, if at all, by saying "no" to his social collective and going it alone. Any theonomous dimension of human existence is precluded to start with. Hence the final polarity stands as between autonomy and heteronomy, to use Paul Tillich's terms.[9] The crucial ethical option then is reduced to that which takes the individual as ultimate and that which takes one or another collective as ultimate.

From its theonomous standpoint, beyond autonomy or heteronomy, Christian ethics would find the secular prescription faulty and delusive. It is faulted in misreading the great either-or as a choice between self and crowd, between nonconformity and social conformity, between solitude and society.

The fundamental trouble from the Christian perspective is not man's puzzlement in ambivalence between crowd or self, but *anomie,* normlessness. Here is the nub of the matter: anomic individuality may be as far from the terms of true community as anomic collectivity. Neither position has adequately coped with the problem of authority which is the converse of the problem of freedom. The deviant, the loner, attempts to overcome alienation and recover his identity by nonconformity, by being sand in the organizational machinery. But he loses his integrity just as pathetically as the strict conformist who is resigned to running with the crowd.[10]

In the conformist's world, the nexus between man and man is the collective. The man who takes the crowd as god and conformity as the way of salvation, however, is yet bedeviled by *anomie.* For the crowd voice is not unanimous, or even a harmony of sound. It is a cacaphony of jarring, dissonant voices. The frantic anxiety noted by William Whyte in the suburban style of life, in the getting and spending with an anxiety chiefly for what the neighbors will think, derives from the fact that the neighbors are by no means of one mind. Public opinion is notoriously fickle. There is no acknowledged Supreme Court to adjudicate the contradictions of taste and preference. "Scientists tell us that . . ." is supposedly definitive: but what they tell us is dictated by commercial interests in advertising. The decrees of the popular polls confuse quantity with quality of opinion and ride up and down with the shifting tides of fickle sentiment. Or "most people would say . . .": this takes Demos for God, and the average for Lord. But even Demos is unstable and unruly in taste, deferring to some elite or other, some ephemeral crowd-hero, or some mass, faceless fear. So the anonymous authorities in the crowd contend with each other, and the conformist, as though in a lifelong fraternity rushing period, does not know to which crowd to give his ultimate pledge. *Anomie* stalks through the mass, sowing confusion.

On the other hand, the problem of *anomie* bedevils the nonconformist as well. Where nonconformity itself is taken as *nomos,* where one runs counter to prevailing morals and mores to try to find one's positive identity in rebellion itself, one is no closer to authentic community. For the true protestant in history, religious or secular, has been one who rebels against a particular perversion of community in the name of a truer community. He is a deviant, not for the sake of deviance, but out of obedience to a higher law now being forgotten or distorted. He is a rebel with a cause more positive than rebellion. He may be out of step with his confreres, but he marches, as Thoreau's phrase put it, "because he hears a different drummer." He may protest one or another tyranny, but if his dissent be prompted by no prior assent to higher authority, he only contributes to anarchy. He is the inauthentic rebel, and stands as far from community as does his conforming neighbor.

At this juncture a fresh consideration of Christian theonomy, transcending autonomy or heteronomy, may prove relevant to our diagnosis and remedy. The norm of theocentric love, responsible to God for neighbor, takes its bearings neither from the crowd as ultimate nor from the private self as ultimate. Therefore it is not predisposed for conformity or nonconformity as the sole path of moral wisdom and the rule of action. *Agape* transcends crowd or self as ultimate. By virtue of its theocentric reference, Christian love has a profoundly corporate concern, but it knows as well a detachment from crowd-conformity. It moves in the crowd with compassion, but also with the serenity of a solitude companioned and monitored by One beyond the crowd. In this regard it embodies something of the mind of Christ. Love moves off from the press of the crowd, in the cultivation of a divine presence in the secret places, in order then to return to the crowd more sensitive to persons and their real needs. *Agape* is free from the tyranny of the collective, but free for corporate responsibility. It is in some such fashion as this, claims the Christian, that *agape* overcomes *anomie* and creates community.

Toward the Integrated Society

It would be false to leave the impression from what has been said that contemporary social scientists are all Thoreaus who have lost sight of the corporate ideal. When we inquire of them about the corporate ideal of community that once—somewhere, sometime—prevailed, has now been lost or eclipsed, and might be sought again, the term most frequently heard is "integration."[11] In the integrated society there is a high degree of cohesion through shared loyalties, a oneness together with the richness of pluralism. The cohesion is willed from within, not imposed from without, as in a totalitarian collective. As Robert Angell puts it: Moral integration is "the ordering of human relations through a common orientation toward shared ends and values."[12] But this is not a homogenized society, whose cohesion is the likeness of the same, and whose consensus is agreement of identical selves. Pluralism is a necessary ingredient in the integrated society. Somehow the centrifugal and the centripetal impulses are to be balanced. As Milton Yinger says:

> Perhaps the central value question can be put in these terms: can the members of an urban society maintain a moving equilibrium that permits change, pluralism, individualism, while avoiding full *anomie,* a high level of conflict, and personal demoralization? And can they at the same time enlarge the circle of shared values, while avoiding coercion and totalitarianism?[13]

This citation of the norm of societal integration would seem to correspond exactly with the terms of Christian community, particularly in its balance of order and freedom. It is Augustine's *civitas,* where the "*concordia* of the members on the common objects of their love" is the equivalent of the consensus of shared values. Yet, on closer look, when one asks what values are shared or what the supreme cohesive center of values is, the answers are prescribed in the flat world view of the social scientist, and appear again to the Christian as faulted by *anomie.*

On one matter, there is common agreement among the students of society we have surveyed: religion, at least as traditionally conceived, is no longer a plausible or compelling center of values around which community can be restored. There is a nostalgic acknowledgment that it once did provide the cohesive loyalty, and a concession that in the present there is something equivalent needed: a binding source of authority, a supreme court of moral appeal, and a sense of abiding significance in moral action. But, sad to say, traditional religion is gone and cannot be restored. All that is left is the perfunctory, empty, mumbo jumbo of church rituals. The thinkers we have examined would probably concur with Robert Lynd:

> Religion, in its traditional form, is a dying reality in current living. Yet vital culture needs emotionally rich common sentiments. . . . American culture, if it is to be creative in the personalities of those who live it, needs to discover and to build prominently into its structure a core of richly evocative common purposes which have meaning in terms of the deep personality needs of the great mass of the people. . . . Needless to say, the theology, eschatology, and other familiar aspects of traditional Christianity need not have any place in such an operating system.[14]

If Christian values, or the norm of Christian community, are no longer viable, what then *are* the values proposed that can command the loyalty requisite to restore a sense of community? Here the answers are varied and uncertain. Some like Robert Nisbet, following Durkheim, in the face of the breakdown of the nuclear family and the rise of the totalitarian state, call for the recovery of the smaller, intermediate cluster of the working group or the guild as the integrating centers. But there is question as to the adequacy of the value these groups embody, if they are economic in intention. A similar prescription is proferred by Erich Kahler, who calls for revived "Communities of Work"—a kind of democratic socialism—as the road to community, avoiding the tyrannies of both communism and capitalism.[15] Others focus on more vaporous ideals: democratic values, humane values, the dignity of man, the sacredness of persons, creativity, creative altruism, productivity, the fulfillment of human potentialities—terms all evoking warm sentiments but lacking in precise content.

It has been the consistent thesis of this volume that in the dialogue between theology and social science, the norm of Christian community need not be relegated in such a cavalier fashion to the bin of oblivion. There may be an authentic answer for the problem of community in the historic Christian traditions, to be listened to afresh, offering answers relevant precisely where the terms of community have been lost, and where the sociologist's prescriptions falter, on the issue of *anomie* and authority.

There may be needed strenuous translation of theological terms, to dislodge their depth meaning from a literalistic sense and the prescientific world view in which they were cast. The effort at translation, though painful, may prove rewarding.

The secular sociologist may have dismissed religious categories simply out of ignorance of tradition, or a misunderstanding of their meanings. Or he may have conscientiously rejected a religious answer to the problem of *anomie* out of a despair with the pluralism of the religious communities. When he turns to ask for *the* religious basis of community, and the keys to the kingdom, he hears many voices in contention for the crown of authority, spokesmen for churches and sects, pontificial or evangelical, each setting up his booth amid the lonely crowd and each claiming exclusively the terms of authentic community and eternal life. *Anomie,* it would seem, haunts the church as much as it does the world.

No blithe Christian prescription can overlook the fissures and contentions prevailing in the institutional expressions of Christianity in the churches of Christendom. At the same time, however, realism requires a fair-minded second hearing of the positive answers given through the churches, the word of the Christian theologians to the problem of community. For emerging from the debate is a strong ecumenical consensus. Its message is that Christian community, as given by God in the order of creation, broken by man in the fall, and subject to God's judgment in social disintegration, may yet be recovered, insofar as men respond to God's grace, in a life of responsible and obedient love. The fruit of such responsible love is an integrated community—centered not in the individual as the ultimate digit nor in the collective, but in the Kingdom of God. The by-product of such loyalty is both the common good and the realization of true identity.

Lest this claim for the relevance of the Christian answer to the problem of community remain a pious platitude, to be consigned to the bin of oblivion where social scientists normally file church pronouncements, it remains now to attempt to document this claim, in an examination of American society in its political, racial, and academic form. Our lead question is to ask whether there be indeed plausible wisdom in *agape* for the *anomie* that troubles the children of men busy in the building of their glorious and pathetic little kingdoms.

NOTES

1. David Riesman, *The Lonely Crowd,* Pt. III, also *Individualism Reconsidered and Other Essays* (The Free Press of Glencoe, Inc., 1954).

2. Riesman, *The Lonely Crowd,* p. 298.

3. William H. Whyte, Jr., *The Organization Man,* p. 443.

4. *Ibid.,* p. 13.

5. Erich Fromm, *The Sane Society, The Art of Loving.*

6. C. Wright Mills, *The Sociological Imagination,* pp. 172, 187, 190–194.

7. Winston White, *Beyond Conformity.* From a Christian point of view, Harvey Cox expresses similar ideas about the emancipation of urbanization in *The Secular City* (The Macmillan Company, 1965).

8. Ralph Waldo Emerson, *Self Reliance,* in *Essays* (Modern Library, Inc., 1944), p. 32.

9. Tillich's three-way distinction between heteronomy, autonomy, and theonomy is explicated in particular in *The Protestant Era* (The University of Chicago Press, 1948), Ch. IV.

10. John Schaar, *Escape from Authority: The Perspective of Erich Fromm* (Basic Books, Inc., 1961), finds this the essential flaw in Fromm's analysis and prescription.

11. Reference is here made to such writers as Robin Williams, *American Society,* Ch. XIV; Milton Yinger, "On *Anomie,*" *Journal for the Scientific Study of Religion,* Vol. III (April, 1964), and *Religion, Society and the Individual* (The

Macmillan Company, 1957); Robert Angell, *Free Society and Moral Crisis;* Robert Nisbet, *The Quest for Community;* and Talcott Parsons, beyond those already alluded to.

12. Angell, *op. cit.,* p. 8.

13. Yinger, "On Anomie," *Journal for the Scientific Study of Religion,* III (April, 1964), p. 173.

14. Robert S. Lynd, *Knowledge for What?,* pp. 238–239. There are similar out-of-hand dismissals of Christianity in Robert M. MacIver (*The Ramparts We Guard,* p. 111), Angell (*op. cit.,* pp. 24–25), Abraham Kaplan (*loc. cit.,* in E. E. Morison [ed.], *The American Style,* p. 6), Erich Kahler (*Man the Measure: A New Approach to History* [Pantheon Books, Inc., 1943] and *The Tower and the Abyss* [The Viking Press, Inc., 1967]), David Riesman, and Karl Mannheim. William Whyte and Clyde Kluckhohn see the loss of community as due to the breakdown of "the Protestant ethic," but in the normative vein find no need or hope for restoring it. The so-called "return to religion" Kluckhohn reads as serving a social and affiliative function, not as the recovery of an inner vertical orientation of life (Kluckhohn, "Shifts in Values," p. 180).

15. Kahler, *The Tower and the Abyss,* Ch. VII.

VII

Christian Community and American Democracy

For the final chapters of the study, it is proposed that we test out the thesis of the earlier chapters in an examination of certain aspects of American life by the light of the norm of Christian community. In particular, three areas chosen are those which serve to illustrate in a vivid way the crisis of community and the relevance of Christian insights. To select the realms of politics, race, and the university by which to measure our theory of community is only a sampling. The examination of the American family and of the American economy, and indeed of the institutional church, would be as fitting. But these matters are bracketed herein, since it is impossible to do justice to every phase of American culture. We select three where the crisis of community is especially evident.

The thesis of this present chapter can be simply stated by use of the analogy of spirit in relation to body. Where democratic political structures and institutions are infused by the spirit of Christian ethics, they embody the qualities of authentic community. The thesis itself is plain; its support is more complex.

At the outset, we need to make clear the faith standpoint from which the relationship of Christianity and democracy is viewed. It is *not* the one, frequently encountered in patriotic rhetoric, of a utilitarian theology where the final faith is put in the American way of life itself and where Christianity is valid only as instrumental to this political god.[1] However solemnly celebrated in presidential inaugural addresses and devoutly held by many who regard themselves as good Christians and good Americans, it is a subtle idolatry when judged from the standpoint of historic Christianity. One may grant that the health of the body politic is sustained by the spirit of Christian ethics without subscribing to this idolatry.

The stance here taken, as previously affirmed, is that of radical monotheism, an ultimate allegiance to the God of the Christian faith and ethically to the norms of his Kingdom. Its corollary is a provisional and relative loyalty to the kingdoms of this world. Such a stance does not mean detachment or aloofness from political obligation. Quite the contrary, the Christian is under mandate from the God of his life to show forth his faith in all the secular spheres of decision and action. Therefore, he will witness to his transcendent faith by strengthening, correcting, renewing the political institutions in which inevitably he moves. But always he will have a Christian perspective on American democratic political institutions rather than a democratic assessment of the Christian faith.

The same matter might be phrased in terms of the Christ-culture polarity earlier mentioned.[2] One common understanding of the relationship of Christianity to democracy characteristic of the Protestant liberal era conceived of Christ as the hero of democratic values, and the God of our fathers deserving of worship insofar as he is the supporter of democratic institutions. This Christ-of-culture position is set aside here as parochial. In its stead, the "transformationist" position is adopted: a Christian's primary allegiance to God in Christ bears the fruit of moral action zealous to transform all the orders of culture by Christian moral norms. So, it is hoped, the health of the body politic will be sustained by a style of choice in allegiance pledged to a source beyond politics itself.

In our consideration of the ideological relationship between the Christian norm of community and American democracy, we are excluding from our purview certain large matters: for one thing, the *historic* connection between Christianity and democracy. This is a complex story retold in many places. The historical debate will probably never be settled between those who see the rise of democracy as a progressive emancipation from the Christian world view and those who see it as flowering from religious roots.[3] Our interest in the current ideological relationship cannot forget its history, of course. The reflections about man in relation to the state on the part of a Calvin or Hooker, or of a Jefferson or Madison, are pertinent perennially. But our primary interest is contemporary.

Also, it should be clear that in speaking of Christian community and American democracy, we explore issues much deeper than those of church-state relations. True, between the lines of the technical, legal, and constitutional problems of church and state there are many issues involved of faith and morality. But the phrase "Christian community" is not identical with the word "church," any more than the phrase "American democracy" coincides with the word "state," as a formal legal institution.

Man's Government Under the Sovereignty of God

The theological premise for the Christian interpretation of political life has already been set forth in earlier chapters.[4] The state is "ordained of God." It is of "the order of creation." These traditional phrases hold good in conveying a universal meaning far beyond the particular local monarchical forms of government in the mind of a Paul or Luther or Calvin who affirmed them. The contemporary meaning is well conveyed by Aristotle's phrase: "Man is by nature a political animal." That is, the state is ordained of God, not as something alien, imposed on man from without, but intrinsic to man, given with his very being as social. Political relations of authority and consent, in greater or less sophistication, are always to be found wherever persons are found in social interaction. The "state" and its authority may be a very simple one, as with a family relationship or the neighborhood P.T.A., or it may be very complex, as with the United Nations. But along the continuum from simple to complex, there is no abrupt breakpoint between a nonpolitical and a political relation, between the absence and presence of a state. Wherever there is lawmaking and law-enforcing authority, which sets the outward terms and conditions of community, there is the state. In the following discussion, therefore, when we refer to the "state," we do not refer in Hegelian style to some huge Thing, a metaphysical entity. The "state" is only a shorthand term to refer to the people in their political relations, as the word "economy" means the people in their economic relations and the "family" the people in their domestic relations.

This conception of the nature of the state as divinely given with human nature is characteristic of orthodox Christianity, both Catholic and Protestant. At Vatican II, the Roman Church reiterated this position in defining the nature of politics: "The political community and public authority are based on human nature and hence belong to an order of things divinely foreordained."[5] The same idea is axiomatic for main-line Protestant thought, honoring the state as divinely ordained and respecting political authority as under God.[6]

There is evident here a sharp contrast between the Christian position on politics and those versions of the "social contract" theory which regard the state in some sense as an "artificial" contrivance of man superseding a nonpolitical "state of nature." For Christian thought, the political community is not a contrivance of human ingenuity. It is given immediately with the original covenant of community. It is an aspect of the "state of nature."

This main-line Christian view is also to be delineated from the radical sectarian doctrine that the state as a "dyke against sin" is an aspect solely of the fallen order, not of the original created order.[7] From this arises the sectarian suspicion of all political power as morally bad, in contrast to the view accepting and acknowledging power as good, and deserving Christian support and participation. The fact that the state is *also* of the fallen order of corruption, as too of the order of redemption, does not obscure from sight its original created goodness.

Love as the Bond of Democratic Community

As we turn now to consider the political institutions of American democracy by the light of Christian community, we presume certain hallmarks of democracy, as it has evolved in recent history. The first is popular sovereignty. "Governments derive their just powers from the consent of the governed." The practices and institutions of representative government, where policy and law must reflect the popular will, are clearly a primal feature of democracy: "government of the people, by the people."

But does government by popular consent and majority rule always lead to community? Does the will of the people prove best "*for* the people"? This moral question inside the political question has been contended for centuries by force of words and arms. Among the many moral justifications advanced for democracy conceived as government by popular consent, the secular and Christian reasons are closely mixed. One clear Christian reason is based on the doctrine of creation: the entrustment of government to the people expresses the common and equal worth of every man as creature of God. Put in the famous words of Colonel Rainborough, of Cromwell's army in seventeenth-century England:

> For really I think that the poorest he that is in England hath a life to live, as the greatest he; and therefore truly, sir, I think it's clear, that every man that is to live under a government ought first by his own consent to put himself under that government.[8]

The battle is perpetually joined between the champions of this democratic faith and the disciples of aristocracy, who would limit popular consent and preempt power for some elite, even behind the facade of democratic political institutions. In this debate, Christianity has never been identified with absolute unqualified democracy, nor can it be. From the standpoint of Christian ethics, there *are* certain limits on universal franchise. Children and illiterates—though surely creatures—should not vote. Criteria of maturity and intelligence are valid qualifications for voting privilege. On the other hand, such arbitrary exclusions as are made on the basis of race, or economic class, or religious persuasion run counter to the moral norm of universality in common creatureliness.

But does popular consent per se assure community? *Vox populi, vox Dei?* In the answers one hears in the history of political philosophy in the West, one may detect a basic division between those who would trust *quantity* of opinion to assure health in the body politic, whose faith is in the god Demos, and those who would rely on *quality* of opinion as the aristocratic principle safeguarding right community in a democracy. It is not a neat division of the house, of course, between devotees of quantity and quality of opinion. Both parties in the debate, from Aristotle on down, recognize the need for a right mixture. But for one who is a radical democrat, there is an implicit assumption that political salvation lies by way of mass judgment, that one comes closer to right policy by counting more noses.

From what has been said earlier, it is evident that one who starts with Christian premises of community would protest this simple trust in Demos. For *anomie* haunts the mass as closely as the few. One note characteristic of close students of the political temper of the twentieth century is the deep suspicion of mass judgment.[9] To Abraham Lincoln's rhetorical question: "Why should there not be patient confidence in the ultimate justice of the people?" one impressive answer is given: "Because the blind lead the blind." The low incidence of responsible participation in a democracy is not a lack of technical means of communication, but a lack of allegiance to moral norms of community, in short, *anomie*. The bedlam of *anomie* is not overcome by adding more voices. It only raises the decibel count. Here is the truth in Kierkegaard's acid dictum: "The crowd is untruth."

This suspicion of Demos is as old as the democratic revolutions themselves. The Founding Fathers feared anxiously the degradation of democracy into "mobocracy," and tried to guard against it by the nurture of public opinion in rational judgment. The *aristoi,* the best, were men of reason who protected democracy from the tyranny of the mass.

A Christian apologetic for democracy similarly upholds the need for the aristocratic quality of opinion. Sheer quantity of popular will may in any one crisis destroy community, even behind the facade of constitutional legality. The peril to community is heightened in the twentieth century, in ways unimagined by the rational gentry of eighteenth-century America, by the mass media of communication which can manipulate the passions and engineer a consensus for the demagogue. "Totalitarian democracy" is more than a phrase: it becomes a present peril unless mass opinion is checked and altered from within by sober and informed judgment.

In the political philosophy of the Enlightenment, the primal moral polarity is between passion and reason. For a Jefferson or a Locke, it is assumed that reason is per se benevolent, and passion self-interested. The passion of the mob is dreaded as "factious," and the cool reason of the aristocrat is trusted as mindful of the common good. In Christianity the primal moral polarity is not so much between reason and passion as it is between self-love and neighbor love, between the passionate and reasoning self directed toward itself versus the passionate and reasoning self directed toward the common good. Here is a distinctively Christian contribution to the problem of democracy. It is not only *rational* public opinion, an informed "consent of the governed" that is prerequisite, but a *benevolent* will in the citizen, the will to universality, that is needful for community. When the citizen exercises his vote out of a will to the common good, defined in terms both of quantity and quality, opting for a party or policy serving the better good of the more inclusive number, then *vox populi* is more likely to be *vox Dei*. Conversely, when he wills *only* his partisan interests, against the common good, then community is endangered or vitiated: *vox populi, vox diaboli*. Political choices on earth, to be sure, are posed never as a neat option between universal and private good, between God and the devil. In any election, or any political choice before the legislature, the ethical options are highly mixed and ambiguous.[10] But within the gray mixture, the more inclusive and benevolent vs. the more exclusive and partisan represents the crucial absolute in the relativity.

Essentially the same matter might be stated in shorthand, using the language of love and justice. "Love is the bond of community."[11] Our leitmotiv is relevant to the maintenance of community within the practice of popular sovereignty. Here taken not as private affection in a unilateral relation but as loyalty to the common good in multilateral relations, love finds its public expression as justice, the kind of justice intended in Reinhold Niebuhr's well-known words: "Man's capacity for justice makes democracy possible."

Love as Safeguard Against Tyranny

The opposite side of the dialectic is suggested in the remainder of Niebuhr's saying: "Man's inclination to injustice makes democracy necessary."[12] Each side of this paradox must be observed. It will not do to try to find the Christian foundation for democracy entirely in its trust that man will seek the common good, alike with his own, out of a pure and disinterested love of his neighbor. For the citizen is not only a creature responding in innocent benevolence to all fellow creatures in the universal peaceful community of Eden. He is also in the fallen order, a sinner among sinners, seeking a private advantage over his neighbor, in a warfare of every man against every man.

This dark aspect of human nature, already treated in our discussion of negative community, has been the special concern of that strand of Christian thought which takes its cue from Augustine.[13] In Protestantism especially, the bearing of the doctrine of human sin upon man's political institutions on earth has been a recurring theme. The claim has been made by many—if not conceded by all—that constitutional democracy in America was founded as much on Calvinism, with its ringing affirmation of the sovereignty of God and the sinful proclivity of man, as upon the Enlightenment with its trust in human rationality and benevolence.[14] Though these theological roots have been largely overlooked by contemporary secular interpreters of democracy, the bearing of Calvinistic insights for the moral worth of democratic institutions is still cogent. Two in particular are suggested here: (1) the doctrine of the sin of man with its political implication of the separation of powers and (2) the doctrine of the sovereignty of God with its implications of a limited state and the transcendent ground of political rights.

First, the separation of powers. The American Constitution is a carefully devised framework of checks and balances among the various centers of power. The executive, legislative, and judicial branches of government have restraints on each other. There are checks between the upper and lower houses and between elected representatives and the populace who elect them. There are dispersions of jurisdiction between federal, state, and local governments. The moral justification for this delicately equilibrated system of countervailing power can hardly be a pragmatic one: it is the least efficient scheme of government imaginable. Its moral logic goes deeper: given man's proclivity to use power to serve his private ends, the common good is better served where this imperialism is restrained in the ground rules of political transaction. In *The Federalist Papers,* it is "faction" that closely threatens community. Every party and branch of government must be held off from other parties, lest the whole of the body politic suffer.

For example, the Constitution prevents the direct rule of the people by the system of staggered elections and relatively long-term tenure for a senator. This is a guard against the "fickle passions" of the populace, in protecting the wisdom and experience of senior representatives. Yet a senator is held accountable, not only by other branches of government, but by his own constituency in due time. Over the long pull, the people's real good is thus better served by this device of indirect democracy, where those elected to office represent the will of the people but are also protected against it. As James Russell Lowell said somewhere, "The Constitution is an obstacle to the whim but not to the will of the people."

When we look at democratic institutions as an expression of negative community,[15] as dikes against sin, it is important to ask: What inner motivation of the members sustains the dike? Is there any *inner* check on partisan animus and the thrusts for power? Part of the answer may be found in the moral stance of contrition and repentance, as these are understood in the Christian faith. To be sure, the spirit of contrition does not normally characterize the political battles of elections or debate on the Senate floor. It is not part of accepted mores for the warrior to be penitent or mournful. He is supposed to assume the stance of St. George attacking the dragon. It would cause some dismay if in a national election, or in a debate in the UN Security Council between the Jews and the Arabs, each side allowed that "the sacrifices of God are . . . a broken and a contrite heart," and publicly confessed its sin in penitence.

Yet there is a political form that contrition can and sometimes does take. The clue is suggested by Reinhold Niebuhr:

> The heedlessness of love, which sacrifices the interests of the self, enters into calculations of justice principally by becoming the spirit of contrition which issues from the self's encounter with God. In that encounter it is made aware of the contingent character of all human pretensions and ideals. This contrition is the socially relevant counterpart of love. It breaks the pride of the implacable contestants and competitors in all human encounters and persuades them to be "kindly affectioned one with another, . . . forgiving one another, even also as God in Christ has forgiven you." (Eph. 4:32) This spirit lies at the foundation of what we define as democracy.[16]

Contrition before God takes political form in action among men who acknowledge the wisdom of the democratic machinery limiting all private imperialisms, especially one's own. It takes concrete form in the willingness of a partisan candidate to criticize and correct his own side by the same standard employed in criticizing the opposing party. Contrition also is bodied forth in the openness of the majority to the wisdom in the minority's dissent, in the minority's obedience to the very law whose enactment it has fought to prevent, in the closing of ranks after an election, in the concessions and compromises of diplomacy—these all mark the presence of a contrite heart and the intimation of universality within partisan strife. Where men acknowledge and obey the structures of countervailing power that limit their own, political decision is redeemed indirectly by contrite love.

In sum, to interpolate Niebuhr's dictum: Man's capacity for justice (as his benevolence to regard the universal good) makes democracy (as the extension of popular sovereignty) possible; man's inclination to injustice (as his will to partisan power) makes democracy (as the diffusion of centers of authority) necessary. The same dialectic could be phrased still another way: Democracy is guarded from anarchy by the inner will to universality. It is guarded from tyranny by checks against thrusts for power of its several parts, acknowledged in contrition before God. Thus, a Christian will to community keeps the precarious equilibrium between freedom and order.

The Transcendent Ground of Political Rights

We have indicated something of the bearing of a vital belief in the sovereignty of God upon the democratic practice of the separation of powers. There is another implication of this doctrine for democracy: the limitation on the power of the state. If indeed "under God," the state may never be allowed by its citizens to preempt ultimate totalitarian power. Transcendent loyalty is the final ground of protest. "We must obey God rather than men."

In the democratic nations of the West the doctrine of the limited power of the state is universally celebrated in its statements of faith and commonly heeded in practice. "The state exists for man; not man for the state." Here is the familiar rebuke in the democratic credo against totalitarian regimes of whatever sort.

The logic of the defense for this limitation of the state is a laissez-faire concept: to secure the inalienable rights and freedoms of the individual. But exactly here arises the dilemma in the democratic dogma. If the final and complete good for which the state exists is presumed to be the rights of man, individualistically conceived, and all policies of government must conduce to this end, what is to preserve community from flying apart into anarchy? If "freedom from" alien constraint is the supreme value, what safeguards the exercise of such freedom from anomic license?

The secular philosophies of the Enlightenment, whether in

the eighteenth or twentieth centuries, cast the case for freedom and rights in terms of a polarity between collectivism and individualism. As Reinhold Niebuhr has discerned, this polarity is read too simply. Its proponent often trips over the antimony within freedom, namely, that freedom "from" is destructive of community unless conjoined with freedom "for" a positive good sought. Likewise, "rights" need to be coupled with "duties" lest the society disintegrate for lack of a cohesive loyalty.

The Christian theory of community is pertinent here at the nexus of the democratic dilemma, for it brings to bear an insight of faith transcending a simple option between individualism and collectivism. "Man does not exist for the state." Granted. But it is fatally incomplete then to affirm that "the state exists for man," if that means radical individualism. In Christian terms the statement should rather be: "The state exists for man-in-community." Then if community means man-under-God, or man responsible to God for neighbor, it becomes not "man against the state," but "man for God against the state." Similarly, it is not the "Free Society" that is the Christian's final good, but the "Responsible Society." What the Christian brings to the debate about the merits and perils of "the democratic way of life," therefore, is a theonomous faith perspective, a theonomy (to use Paul Tillich's terms) that transcends the simple option between anomic autonomy and tyrannical heteronomy.[17]

This thesis may be supported by reference to the constitutional rights of American democracy. The long, bitter struggle for the establishment of rights in the West, since Magna Carta, has been championed by those whose claim for rights, whether economic, political, or religious, was always from obligation to a higher good served. So in the present, the exercise of these hard-won rights claimed against the state's alien usurpation conduce to the health of the state only if practiced out of loyalty to a transcendent authority. The rights of freedom of speech, press, and assembly are viable in practice only where citizens speak and print what in conscience is the truth as they see it. This right is not boundless. The outer limits are set by laws against libel and slander, themselves witness that such rights are relative to a norm of truthtelling in community. But the *inner* limits on the exercise of these rights, that quite evade the reach of laws, inhere in the person's will to seek and say the truth of the matter.

Likewise the right of peaceable assembly and petition for redress of grievances assumes that some common good, currently abridged, must be pursued. The right of property is constitutionally assured to private citizens. But it is presumed that this economic right is exercised out of a will to the commonweal, however variously conceived. This norm derives from the long-established Christian ethical heritage, Catholic and Reformed: private property for common use.

Likewise, the claim for the rights of conscience in freedom of worship against any governmental proscription depends for its viability upon a higher obedience: "We must obey God rather than men." Where freedom to worship is neglected in practice, or where it is extended out so far into a freedom of indifference that it becomes of no moment whether men worship or not, then the right to worship may itself be endangered or lost by neglect of its use.

Any one of these sacred rights, then, is a precarious good. Community teeters at the edge of anarchy in every democratic political decision, whether it be a zoning regulation of a city council, a Supreme Court decree on racial legislation, a presidential election, or a university dean's ruling about parietal hours for students. From the standpoint of Christian ethics, what tips the society in each case toward community is a theocentric basis of the exercise of right, countervailing every claim and extension of right with an intention of duty, running the risk for every freedom granted out of a trust that it will be responsibly used. Here is the inner Christian basis of democracy, the answer of *agape* to *anomie*.[18]

Conscience, Compromise, and Community

Any statement of Christian norms for the political order is likely to be cast in terms of "glittering generalities." Certain prized values are observed in a fixed constellation, where no one star jars another. The World Council of Churches, for instance, affirms that "the Christian seeks a responsible society in which there is a genuine respect for persons, freedom, peace, justice for all, and a due restraint of power."[19] The ritual of saluting the American flag calls the citizen to honor "one nation, indivisible, with liberty and justice for all."

Such high and resounding moral ideals preside over political processes as transcendent regulative norms and final ends, but they do not operate directly in the traffic of actual political decision. For in practice these ideals collide more often than coincide; the choices of politics are choices *among* them, not choices for or against them altogether. The pursuit of liberty may run counter to justice; the pursuit of justice may curtail liberty. Or the liberty of some must sometimes be bought at the price of the liberty of others. Justice for a minority collides with justice for another minority. Though in the heavenly city there may be liberty and justice for all, in the political economy of scarcity which characterizes politics on earth, the choices are always between proximate and partial realizations, between competing values, interests, needs, groups, and parties, where men have to content themselves with half a loaf.

Politics is the "art of the possible." To be relevant, ethical theory must relate the pure to the possible. It is a false stance, though one commonly encountered among Christian moralists, which regards politics as "dirty," the realm of tricky deals and sordid manipulations. It is not surprising that when he confronts its moral muddle, the response of the Christian purist is either to withdraw, to protect his saintly virtue from contamination, or to march with a great crusade to clean up city hall or "the mess in Washington," and establish a holy commonwealth.[20]

In common purist talk, the word "integrity" has a fine ring, the word "compromise" a bad one. The man of integrity is one whose allegiance to principle will not be swerved by low considerations. He does not compromise his principles out of a passion for power. He would rather be right than President. Compromise, on the other side, is read to mean sheer expediency, the machinations of the "operator" who holds no principles save what is opportune for his own power-seeking. He would rather be President than right.

Such a notion of the bearing of Christian ethics on politics is at best an inept and sentimental idealism. It quite overlooks the hard ambiguities of political processes, and is faulted to start with, even in its theory of community. The usual stereotypes are here set aside for a more exact understanding of the meanings of integrity and compromise.

Christian realism in ethics drives between the naïveté of purism and the cynicism of sheer expediency, to find Christian integrity within compromise.[21] Integrity in political choice does not mean the protection of antiseptic purity, but a cultivated, prudent capacity to choose the better over the worse, since the best is always closed off. Compromise means simply the sacrifice of one value out of allegiance to a preferred value. Compromise is the very stuff of politics, for political choice is always a tangled mixture among competing goods, always a matter of value priorities. The ethical question is not *whether* to compromise, but *how*.

From the most simple politics of a family conference about vacation plans to the complex maneuvering in a national political convention, it is evident that the process of compromise is necessary. The priorities may be on several incommensurate planes. Yet they converge at the nexus of choice. There is the *value* dimension of compromise, for one thing. At every hand, men are forced to forgo some values in preference for others, compromising on sleep and energy, for example, in devotion to exhausting causes. There is the *time* dimension, for another, where it is necessary to sacrifice or risk an immediate good out of preference for a far-off one. Conversely, one may compromise an interest of posterity to seize a present value, deciding that a bird in hand is worth two in the bush. Prudence in politics involves skill in the art of timing, an instinct for the propitious time. There is also the *social* dimension of compromise. Not only what values and when, but whose? The interests of some must be compromised to serve others. Peter must be robbed to pay Paul, but in such fashion that Peter is beguiled into thinking that he loses nothing. To get a bill passed in Congress on tax, or tariff, or immigration, or reapportionment legislation, under the cloud of oratory proclaiming the good of all, the most intricate maneuvering of compromise is required, taking away a little here to add something there, in order to achieve a rough and proximate justice. Or the problem of compromise may come in the form of collision between principles on the value scale and interests on the social scale. In an election, how ought a candidate to declare himself on a controverted issue where his personal persuasion runs athwart the belief of the power bloc whose votes he must have to get elected? The same problem dogs him when he has won: in voting, his obligation to his conscience to vote on the intrinsic merits of a bill vs. his obligation as representative of his constituency to vote their way. How far ahead of his constituency can he move without committing political suicide?

It is relatively easy to pose the problem and to dissect the anatomy of the problem of compromise, but quite more difficult to delineate the Christian norms for better compromise vs. worse. But one may draw from our previous discussion a few major guidelines.

The presiding norm to guide compromise is the norm of Christian community animated and sustained by love. Christian love is the norm of choice. It is relevant to the ambiguities of mixed and gray choices, seeking as it does in the jungle of ambiguities not perfect community, but proximate community. Under the narrow conditions posed by the power structures of politics, since perfect community is foreclosed, the alternative is not absolute chaos. Nor need choice be made by tossing a coin. There is yet the better to be chosen over the worse. Integrity in compromise appears in the imagination of moral insight choosing that option closer to Christian community. The worse compromise is the decision that sacrifices the common good to serve self-interested pride and power.

A few instances may serve to illustrate. In an election, does Christian love exact that the candidate speak the truth, the whole truth, and nothing but the truth? The form that Christian love takes for the campaigner would be neither full candor nor downright deceit. Discretion, silence, equivocation, the diplomatic dodge in the press conference—these are prudent compromises of the full truth, legitimate to adopt where the long-range ends of better community are served. To be sure, there must be a general conformity of means and ends, if not a strict one. Equivocation itself cannot be the rule of political speech, for this can be self-defeating. Deliberate misrepresentation can create in time a credibility gap destructive of a community of trust. But withal, the prudent politician who will discreetly cut across a small corner on the whole lot of honesty to serve a larger good is making the better compromise. A politician of the moral style of a Senator Joseph McCarthy, on the other hand, who engaged in wholesale deceit and lying out of self-interested power-seeking, even behind the front of legal propriety, was patently involved in the worse compromise. It is the basic polarity between universality and partiality, set in the law of Christian love, that makes the crucial moral difference.

Comparably, in international relations, the art of diplomacy, in achieving a measure of viable community out of a collision of national interests, entails a delicate discretion in the representation of truth. The self-defensive lie, which must sacrifice the truth to save its own face in a paroxysm of national self-righteousness, prevents peaceful accord. The other-defensive lie, the diplomatic device that allows the opposing nation to save face, may accomplish a peaceful settlement.

A quite different kind of political dilemma involving compromise in choice appears in the collision between the good of persons and the good of laws or principles by which people operate. Deep in the democratic conscience is the recognition of the moral wisdom of government by law, to which rulers and ruled are alike subject. The traffic of daily life requires a tacit acknowledgment that the good of community requires enactment and enforcement of laws. But of course in practice, a particular law may violate the good of persons. The agonizing choice then confronts an administrator or juryman, between compromising the well-being of this person to a good law, or taking exception to the law to serve the person. How does the Christian norm of community assist in such a moral quandary?

No community can operate anomically. Laws are its sinews.

Yet it is also plain that no existing system of positive law can be sufficiently sensitive to the individual variations and needs and deserts of its members to do them full justice. For law is by nature impersonal, squeezing persons into cases, treating "thous" as "its." Law is also conservative, static, laden with anachronism. Legislation enacted to meet new conditions quickly becomes archaic and sacrifices the need of present persons to past precedent. A legally proper decision of the courts may involve a monstrous miscarriage of justice for particular people.

In the complex process of enactment, judicial interpretation, and administration of laws, there can be no unexceptionable rule that can adjudicate love's claim, in the inevitable collision between persons and systems. It will not do to say: laws should always be abrogated to serve persons, any more than one can say: the law must be followed to the letter, no matter how many persons must suffer thereby. The prudent pragmatism of Christian ethics will now bend the law to favor this person or that, but then hold persons to the requirements of the law without fear or favor, compromising this person's need for a common good the law conserves. The guiding norm in all this uncertainty is Christian community. A judge in the traffic court refuses to fix a ticket for a wealthy friend. He serves Christian community through strict adherence to law. A judge in a juvenile court takes exception to the letter of the law to parole the delinquent thief, twelve years old, standing before him, risking thereby neighborhood property. He too serves Christian community through sacrificing the property laws he has sworn to uphold for one person's potential growth into responsible citizenship.

In the Christian norm of community, then, may be found the basis for both a conservative and a revolutionary stance of response to the prevailing laws of the day. There is a strong conservative strand in Christian ethical theory, past and present, so much so that some contemporary Christians feel that it is by charter uncongenial to the revolutionary impulses shaking the foundations of world culture.[22] The stability of law and order are hallmarks of the Christendom of feudal and bourgeois times, compromising equality and justice for the poor and needy to serve the propertied and pious. On the other hand, the prophetic strand of Christian ethical theory has inspired many a major revolution, overturning the old order in the name of a common justice. It was such prophetic obedience to a higher law than the British crown which sparked the American Revolution, claiming the right of the people "to alter or abolish" the existing forms of government. The same conscience for community inspired in the nineteenth century the Christian Social Gospel movement for industrial reform, defying those property laws which turned aside the needy from the gate and trod on the poor. Again, in mid-twentieth century, it is a Christian impulse for racial justice that has challenged existing segregation laws and customs, in the civil rights revolution. The stable structure of laws in any one era, then, deserves the obedience of the Christian, as he seeks the city whose builder and maker is God. But where these laws transgress his ultimate allegiance, the Christian will challenge and defy them, in revolution, out of obedience to the One who makes all things new.

NOTES

1. For careful assessments of this pattern of belief, see William Lee Miller, "American Religion and American Political Attitudes," in James Ward Smith and Leland Jamison (eds.), *Religious Perspectives in American Culture,* Vol. II: Religion in American Life (Princeton University Press, 1961), and *Piety Along the Potomac* (Houghton Mifflin Company, 1964). See also Robert Bellah, "Civil Religion in America," *Daedalus* (Winter, 1967); Will Herberg, *Protestant—Catholic—Jew* (Doubleday & Company, Inc., 1955, rev. 1960); and Kenneth Underwood, *Protestant and Catholic* (The Beacon Press, 1957). All these thinkers detect an American national "religion" to which historic faiths are supportive.

2. See H. Richard Niebuhr, *Christ and Culture.*

3. Classic studies, such as Ralph Gabriel, *The Course of American Democratic Thought* (The Ronald Press Company, 1940), H. Richard Niebuhr, *The Kingdom of God in America,* R. B. Perry, *Puritanism and Democracy* (The Vanguard Press,

Inc., 1944), James Hastings Nichols, *Democracy and the Churches,* are but a few that trace the story. The relationship of seventeenth-century English Puritanism and of Deism and the Enlightenment to the political thought of the Founding Fathers has been of persisting fascination for historians.

4. See pp. 17–25 above.

5. The "Pastoral Constitution on the Church in the Modern World," in William Abbott (ed.), *The Documents of Vatican II,* p. 284.

6. See, for instance, the statement of the World Council of Churches Geneva Conference: *Christians in the Technical and Social Revolutions of Our Time,* pp. 97 ff.

7. See Thomas G. Sanders, *Protestant Concepts of Church and State* (Holt, Rinehart and Winston, Inc., 1964), for a historic typology of the main positions on this matter.

8. A. S. P. Woodhouse (ed.), *Puritanism and Liberty, Being the Army Debates (1647–9) from the Clarke Manuscripts* (The University of Chicago Press, 1951), p. 53.

9. This conviction is shared by such divergent thinkers as Walter Lippmann, *The Public Philosophy* (The New American Library, 1956); Sebastian de Grazia, *The Political Community: A Study in Anomie;* Glenn Tinder, *The Crisis of Political Imagination* (Charles Scribner's Sons, 1964); Robert Angell, *Free Society and Moral Crisis.*

10. President Kennedy was fond of a quote from Lord Morley: "Politics is one long second best, where the choice often lies between two blunders."

11. Sebastian de Grazia's study of American democracy comes to the same conclusion in his Coda: "The theologian is right. Why not admit it? More than anything else, the world needs love. . . . A political community exists among men who regard each other as brothers. But they will not think of themselves as a brotherhood until they have and avow filial love and faith for their ruler and for their God. If they have no faith in their rulers or if they allow opposing directions to sway them from the commandment of love, they have no political community; they have *anomie*" (*op. cit.,* pp. 187, 189).

12. Reinhold Niebuhr, *The Children of Light and the Children of Darkness* (Charles Scribner's Sons, 1944), p. xi.

13. The major contributor in American thought to the recovery of Christian anthropology has been Reinhold Niebuhr. *The Nature and Destiny of Man* has had a wide influence in the development of the so-called school of "Christian realism" in political theory. His *The Children of Light and the Children of Darkness* explores the bearing of Christian anthropology on democracy. See Harry P. Davis and Robert C. Good (eds.), *Reinhold Niebuhr on Politics* (Charles Scribner's Sons, 1960).

14. James Bryce, for example, noted that "there is a hearty Puritanism in the view of human nature which pervades the instrument of 1787. It is the work of men who believed in original sin, and were resolved to leave open for transgressors no door which they could possibly shut" (*The American Commonwealth,* 3d ed. [The Macmillan Company, 1893], I, 299 ff.). See Nichols, *op. cit.,* Ch. I. Madison, a Calvinist, describes the perils of faction arising from sin in *The Federalist Papers,* X.

Many instances could be cited from Puritan authors who trace the necessity of government to man's sin. Richard Baxter, for example: "The vitiousness of men hath made government now of double necessitie to what it would be if men were innocent, when men are wolves to one another, and the weaker can keep nothing that the stronger hath a mind to" (*Holy Commonwealth* [London, 1659], p. 52).

15. See pp. 56–58 above.

16. Davis and Good (eds.), *op. cit.,* p. 158.

17. Paul Tillich, *Love, Power, and Justice.*

18. Of the numerous discussions of the relationships of Christianity and the exercise of democratic rights, the following few are especially pertinent: H. Richard Niebuhr, "The Idea of Covenant and American Democracy," *Church History,* Vol. XXIII (1954), pp. 126–135; H. Richard Niebuhr, "The Protestant Movement and Democracy in the United States," in J. W. Smith and A. L. Jamison (eds.), Religion in American Life, Vol. I: *The Shaping of American Religion* (Princeton University Press, 1961); John Hallowell, "The Nature of Government in a Free Society," in Z. K. Matthews (ed.), *Responsible Government in a Revolutionary Age;* Carl Becker, *Freedom and Responsibility in the American Way of Life* (Alfred A. Knopf, Inc., 1945); Joseph Tussman, *Obligation and the Body Politic* (Oxford University Press, 1960); Walter Berns, *Freedom, Virtue, and the First Amendment* (Louisiana State University Press, 1957).

19. Official Report of the World Conference on Church and Society, *Christians in the Technical and Social Revolutions of Our Time,* p. 111.

20. In the party platform of the Theocratic Party of the United States, it is affirmed that neither divorcées nor lawyers should be allowed to hold public office, presumably because they are immoral and anti-Christian. See William Lee Miller, *Piety Along the Potomac,* for a sharp indictment of Protestant moralism in politics.

21. There are relatively few good studies of compromise from the standpoint of Protestant Christianity. A famous treatment of the issue is Lord Morley's essay *On Compromise* (London: Macmillan & Co., Ltd., 1886). T. V. Smith's *Ethics of Compromise and the Art of Containment* (Starr King Press Book, Beacon Press, 1956) is entirely pragmatic. A rejoinder to his position from a Christian standpoint is to be found in John Hallowell, *The Moral Foundations of Democracy* (The University of Chicago Press, 1954), Ch. II. A perceptive analysis of compromise in politics by Senator Eugene McCarthy is his essay in Robert M. MacIver (ed.), *Integrity and Compromise: Problems of Public and Private Conscience,* (Harper & Brothers, 1957). From a distinctly Protestant Christian standpoint, Edward LeRoy Long, Jr., *Conscience and Compromise: An Approach to Protestant Casuistry* (The Westminster Press, 1954), outlines the issues clearly. See also some of the Occasional Papers of the Experimental Study of Religion and Society (Raleigh, N.C., 1966–1967). Much of the literature in the contextualist ethics debate deals with the problem of compromise in other terms.

22. This theme was intensely debated in the World Council of Churches Geneva Conference of 1966.

VIII

Christian Community and Racial Strife

In the latter part of the twentieth century, the most urgent and baffling domestic problem in American society is by all odds that of race relations. The riots in the ghettos of American cities, as expected turmoils following the summer solstice, the assassinations and mounting violence, the rise of the Black Power movement and the white backlash, the marches on Washington, the debates in Congress, the litigation in the courts, have prompted sober prophecies of a domestic civil war ahead. Certainly these are clear signs of revolutionary change. The outer seething unrest, the bloody riots, and the bloodless legal and legislative combats mark an internal shift within the conscience of American society in the understanding of the terms of community under which black and white are to live together.

Mass media, especially the instruments of instant communication with the all-seeing eye of the roving TV camera, have given the racial crisis a high visibility. Whether it be the ghetto riots, the bleak poverty of the Alabama sharecropper, or the funeral services of Martin Luther King, Jr., and the police treatment of the poor people's march on Washington, racial strife is exposed to public view and subject to minute analysis by the social scientist. What are the causes of racial tension and civil disorder? Every imaginable kind of explanation is offered by presidential commissions[1] and the teams of visiting analysts in the field. Psychological, political, economic, ecological, legal, even physiological factors that make up the dense texture of social interaction are probed and computed. Many true reasons are given, in cause-effect sequences, for our racial disorder.

Our concern herein is with the inner ethical issues in the struggle. Though of much lower visibility, they are factors as crucial as are the outer political and economic ones. The collisions in the streets and the litigations in the courts are expressions of "conflicting valuations" in the heart of America, as Gunnar Myrdal pointed out in his classic study. The loves and hates, the aspirations and dreads, the suspicions and trusts that make up the inner dynamics of community: these become the special province of Christian ethical analysis.

Looked at in this light, it is evident that the relations studied are not simply interracial. The black-white aspect of the relations are crisscrossed by all sorts of interpersonal, nonracial factors; national, domestic, cultural, aesthetic, economic affiliations and antipathies constitute circles of loyalty overlapping the racial ones. Because persons are always more than cases of color, in continual traffic with one another, a purely racial analysis of race relations is a false abstraction.

Relevant Norms of Christian Community

In this survey, we venture to measure the trends of the current racial scene in America, such as are described by social scientist or journalist, against the Christian moral norm of community. As soon as one probes in depth into the tangled web of factors, it becomes apparent that the *motifs* earlier discerned in American society—*anomie,* the loss of community, alienation, anonymity, the fierce and fanatic attempts to recover community, the hypocrisies and deceits, the mixture of courage and cynicism, of kindness and cruelty—constitute the inner dynamics of race relations in America. The meaning of all this is illumined by Christian categories. We should recall briefly the salient elements in the Christian norm of community, theological and ethical, germane to the immediate issue of race.[2]

Man's corporate life is lived, when viewed in Christian terms, under the constant and concurrent action of the sovereign will of God, whose love creates, governs, and redeems man's life. The order of creation, given with every new birth and new day, is the good order of equality and diversity of creatureliness. The infinite variety of sexual, physical, psychic, and ethnic differences is "given" and good, as are the shared gifts and limits of common mortality. Man's proper response to the Creator is a grateful acceptance of the unity and differences of creation and a stewardship of that order in moral actions that cherishes and keeps intact this original community.

Man's corporate life is also lived, however, "in the Fall," where men, abusing their created freedom, corrupt the order of creation and attempt to establish community on sinful terms. This corruption of life is pervasive of all man's circles of neighbor relations, but it is particularly apparent in his racial intercourse. Here man through his will to power attaches merit to the special aspect of skin color as a criterion of value. Radical egocentricity becomes ethnocentrism. Pride, as the substitution of the idol of ethnic self-love for the theocentric love of creation, is the root of the trouble. When "whiteness" is taken as a criterion of worth, the neighbor of another color is judged inferior, the original created community is befouled in the internal springs of action, and outer actions then follow which extend this disorder. The peace of the order of creation is turned into the warfare of race against race, clan against clan. There develop out from the internal wills to power all the demonic cultural institutions, "superpersonal forces of evil"—chattel slavery, segregation, the ghetto, apartheid, etc.—which assume a kind of power independent of the wills of both those who maintain them and those who are victims of them. This is the racial "fall" of man.

Such human disorder involves negative community, the structures of law that keep men in a kind of outer peace with each other by holding them off from each other. This is the meaning of "life under the law," which requires the state as a "dyke against sin." To the Lordship of God as Judge, appearing in this negative form, the response of the Christian is the acknowledgment in contrition of his sin of pride and racial prejudice, and his acceptance of the necessity of the law's restraint of the outer forms of injustice on the part of his neighbors as well as himself, in all the ways that prevent and punish man's inhumanity to man.

Thirdly, and simultaneously, the Christian lives in the faith that there is an order of grace and redemption. Present in every human circumstance, however tragic, is God's gracious *agape* impelling men toward the reconciliation of the estranged and the reunion of the separated. Jesus Christ is the supreme paradigm of this grace of God, the unique exemplar of love. Out of confidence in such reprieves of grace as in Christ and through the Spirit that have forgiven and restored man to newness of life, the Christian is prompted to a like forgiveness of his neighbor and to works of reconciliation restoring community. The classic drama of alienation and reconciliation is relived in the daily drama of men's corporate racial life. The lineaments of God's rule are traced in man's earthly decisions of life in the inner-city ghetto, in open-housing covenants, in high court decisions, in local good-neighbor councils, in the patient sufferings and the fierce uprisings of the oppressed.

The Old Order: Paternalism and Segregation

The current revolution in race relations is pitched against the power of tradition and the inertia of custom. For the large part, men do things the way they have done things, without asking why. The customs of race relations even in the present inevitably reflect the memories of chattel slavery, the Civil War and Reconstruction, segregation, and paternalism. Even while men try to escape their history, to shake off their memories and set new terms of community, their history shadows them.

The long, tragic story of our racial history[3] perdures into the present in a certain fixed pattern of the terms of relation of Negro and white, presumed by the inertia of long usage to be right and good, that we may call *paternalism*. It is that syndrome of attitudes and customs, laws and institutions, which, though challenged and rapidly being overthrown in the Negro revolt, still stands as normative as the Southern way of life, taken for granted as the model of good community. In a New South city, in the textile or tobacco plant, in the domestic economy of suburban Richmond, Memphis, Atlanta—this is the prevailing pattern of peaceful community. Furthermore, this way of life has moved North, with the Negro migration, into the cities of the Northeast and Midwest.

The inner terms of paternalistic relations, as suggested by the word, are basically that the optimum benefits of community are realized when the superior white man takes care of the inferior Negro, and the Negro works for the white man. The relation is one of reciprocal economic interdependence, each looking after the other. The moral virtues sustaining the transaction are taken from the language of Christian ethics: love, charity, kindness, concern, obedience, faithfulness, patience, long-suffering—familiar Biblical virtues. The mechanics of interaction in the paternalistic power structure are oiled by the etiquette of gentle speech and manners: the white housewife is kind to her Negro maid and gives her cast-off clothing; the white boss may be tolerant of the shortcomings of the colored men on his crew, the Negro maid solicitous of the creature comforts of "Miss Mary" and "Miss Margaret." For the white man, the meaning of the word "good" in the phrase "He's a good Negro" connotes patience, contentment, good cheer, docility, and respect for his superiors. In fact, on its morally better side, there is genuine mutual personal affection and concern that permeate the paternalistic arrangement and make it in one sense a true expression of Christian community.

On its dark underside, however, the good of paternalism is despoiled by the sin of racial pride. The affection of white for Negro is tainted by white self-love, and its charity poisoned by condescension. White courtesy becomes not the disinterested regard for the neighbor as equal, but is conditional on the Negro's keeping his inferior place. Let him dare forget the basic premise that the white man's floor is the Negro's ceiling, let him once get uppity and claim equality in power, and the white man's courtesy can quickly turn to arrogance and suspicion. The Negro should keep in his place. Here, incidentally, is where paternalism, morally speaking, is a false analogy, for in a good family, the concern of a father is that his children should not stay children but grow into maturity and independence.

On his side, the Negro member of the paternalistic relation, denied his right to equality, is tempted or forced to assume the Uncle Tom role, a dissembling unction adopted to survive in a white man's world. Behind his deferential speech and grinning face presented to the white man lie a deep resentment and hostility. The terms of community are not the open, honest terms of genuine trust, but the hypocritical, sly, guarded deceits of suspicion, however much each side claims to "know" the other. The relations may be those of close physical proximity, at factory bench, or farmhouse, or kitchen, but even this close community is, inwardly speaking, a broken one of strangers, alienated from each other by the line drawn by white pride, intended to separate forever white superiority from Negro inferiority.

The outer terms of paternalistic community are fixed by the walls of segregation. They represent the extension of the inner private walls of pride and power out into public custom and legal form. In the syllogism of the moral logic of segregation, the major premise is, of course, the constitutional principle of the 14th and 15th amendments, the "equal protection of the laws." The minor premise is that separation by race is not inherently unequal, and that "separate and equal" is a viable formula for the conclusion, agreeable to all, of good community.

Nearly a century of American experience has proved the falsity of this logic. The Supreme Court decision of 1954, overthrowing *Plessy* vs. *Ferguson,* affirmed a point that should have been self-evident, that "separate educational facilities are inherently unequal."[4] Separate and equal in theory became separate and unequal in practice in every sector of common life. For the formula was administered not mutually but by the powerful white majority. Segregation has served to break community, to widen the gap between the powerful and the powerless, to intensify the resentment and distrust that separated neighbors from each other both in spirit and in social space.

The Crisis of Conscience

The "American dilemma," defined by Gunnar Myrdal as the gap between the American moral creed of freedom and equality and the practice of oppression and inequality, has only become intensified since he defined and documented it a quarter century ago. Speaking in Christian theological terms, one may translate this dilemma into terms of the contradiction between the remembered order of creation, the "original" community of equality-in-diversity and mutual accord, and the disordered, broken community in which men live in fear and hostility. The deep sense of guilt is plainly a sign of the tension between the order of creation and the order of the fall in man's soul. His profession of allegiance to Christian and democratic ideals puts the white American at profound odds with himself in his racially prejudiced actions. So acute is this moral self-contradiction that it becomes intolerable to bear, unless it be covered over by fronts and defenses, justifications and rationalizations, wherein he tries to close the self-contradiction, shove his guilt down below sight, and hide his sin with the cloaks of virtue.[5] So, for example, the white man in pride will ascribe the inferior performance of the Negro to an innate racial trait, rather than to the inferior cultural circumstance in which the white establishment has forced the Negro to live, thus shifting the fault from himself to the other. Or he will defend restrictive covenants and resist open-housing laws in the name of freedom. ("A man should be free to sell to whomever he wants.") But of course the intention behind that statement is not for the genuine freedom of anyone to live wherever he will, but for the exclusion of the prospective Negro neighbor. Racial prejudice even defends itself with the language of personal love ("I'm very fond of our maid. She's just like one of the family.") to cover resistance to measures assuring social justice and genuine equality for the Negro minority.

Thus, in sum, a Christian judgment on the paternalistic terms of community is that its peace is kept at the price of injustice, that behind the facade of amiable accord lurk prejudice and deep discord. However much its asperities are softened by personal goodwill, however much acts of Christian kindness can penetrate the chinks in the system, paternalism and segregation deny Christian community.

The New Order: Integration and Equality

As measured by the norm of Christian love, and under the judgment of God, the peace of the old order has been tried and found wanting. It is now being disrupted, giving way to the new order present in the civil rights revolution. Inevitably the mode of change is far from gradual and peaceful. So entrenched in power is the dominant white Establishment, so well guarded its ramparts with its ideology of "good" reasons, so strong is the inertia of custom and so rare the voices of courage and conscience, that the new order comes only against stolid resistance and by violent upheaval.

The terms of community in the new order are those of equality, freedom, and justice. To realize these goods, those in the vanguard of the civil rights revolution are obliged to break the false peace of a segregated, paternalistic society in the name of the equal justice which is the precondition for the authentic peace of Christian community, where men can be together in the true sense only because they are on a par of equal power.

The outer history of the Negro revolt in the mid-century decades starts with the moves toward equal rights and integration through the efforts of the NAACP and other "liberal" organizations through the courts, and the student protests in public places. These efforts in which Negro and white joined forces produced notable gains for equality in the public sector. The precondition for political and economic power for the Negro became more and more firmly established in law. But the gap widened between the formal rights guaranteed the Negro in legal interpretation of the Constitution and his real economic and educational opportunities. School desegregation was grudging, reluctant, and tardy. Fifteen years after *U.S.* vs. *Brown,* only about 12 percent of the public schools in the whole of the South were integrated. And the gap between white America's affluence and Negro poverty continued to widen.

The 1950's saw mounting Negro revolt, direct action in student sit-ins, boycotts, marches, and Freedom Rides. The voice of Negro leadership became more insistent, demanding equal civil rights, in the courts, in the schools, in employment policies, in public housing. Where these rights were not yielded by the white majority, Negro leaders threatened reprisal. Currently, in the late '60s, in the face of "the whips and scorns of time, the oppressor's wrong, the proud man's contumely . . . the law's delay"—the new Negro will wait no longer. He demands equality *now*.

Of major significance for our Christian interpretation of race relations is the thought of Martin Luther King, Jr., the eloquent spokesman for and to the Christian conscience of America.[6] His nurture in the Southern Baptist Church, his advanced training in theology, his pastoral experience in Alabama, his courageous and charismatic leadership of the civil rights movement through the Southern Christian Leadership Conference, made him deeply Christian in his total orientation. His ethical theory can be best understood as a novel combination of ingredients: from liberal Protestantism he drew a confident hope in his dream for the future, and the power of love to appeal to the good in man; from Reinhold Niebuhr a healthy realism about the stubborn power of sin in the form of white prejudice, and the necessity for the use of countervailing power to rescue love from impotence; from Gandhi a strategy of nonviolence as a mass political tool to be used against entrenched power; and from his Southern Baptist heritage an evangelical fervor and a warm personal concern.[7]

For King, Christian love means nonviolence. Its validity derives partly from its conformity to the character of God's love in Christ, but much more from its success in turning the enemy into friend.[8] The intent of the nonviolent form of witness is to appeal to the conscience of the white man and shame him into granting or conceding rights, or at least into withholding the retaliatory backlash that Negro violence would evoke.

In hindsight, the wisdom of King's ethic is difficult to weigh. Many criticized his method, on his own terms, pointing out that it did not avail. His nonviolence was beamed toward the Christian conscience in the white man. But what if that conscience becomes desensitized by its schooling in the violence of TV and the affluence of suburbia? Even before his death, it was said, his crusade was faltering and his technique irrelevant.[9] Many of the young Negro leaders in the civil rights movement turned with greater or less candor toward advocating violence as the only way to achieve justice. Yet, on the other side, there is no doubt that through King's leadership, and as much out of his death as his life, more was gained for community than for chaos. With the growing support of the liberal white leadership, much of it coming from the Christian churches, political and economic advances for Negroes were marked. The degree of equalization of countervailing power may have been discouragingly slight when measured against King's dream of full equality and full freedom, but the conscience of white America *was* profoundly moved, and its political actions reflected the conversion to an appreciable degree. In the long perspective of history, King's way may well prove to have been morally wiser than the way of his critics and opponents.

Through the crusades of King and many others, the middle decades of the twentieth century saw genuine gains in the realization of Christian community in America's race relations. Prophets of doom and crisis could not overlook the progressive desegregation of public schools, the election and appointment of Negroes to high public office in local, state, and federal government, the integration of military life, the increased power of the Negro bloc vote. These all represented movements into the mainstream. The ablest Negro youths, a crucial though tiny minority, were welcomed increasingly in America's best universities and colleges: their experience in integration augured well for the role they would play in the future. The gradual acceptance of the terms of integration in the public and private sectors of life, both North and South, provided the stance of equality whereby the relations could shift easily from being interracial to interpersonal. In all these ways the order of grace and redemption, the reconciliation of man with man, became evident.

Yet the picture remains morally mixed, as the order of sin corrupts even the gains of the order of redemption. The liberal hope for the gradual movement from the old order to the new, from segregation to integration, in the progressive domestication of the dream of Christian community, has been shattered by new, dark forces of disorder and destruction, new polarizations of power. The current mood is more than a tempered hope or a petulance with the tardiness of progress. It is a mood of crisis and apocalyptic urgency, and for many one of despair and dread.

The summer riots of the 1960's jolted severely the liberal's confidence, if not complacency; for what he read as progress, as movements into the mainstream, the Negroes read angrily as mere token gestures, drastically insufficient. It became apparent that the gap between dream and fact was not closing but widening. As the Kerner Report summarized the temper of things in 1967:

> By 1967, whites could point to the demise of slavery, the decline of illiteracy among Negroes, the legal protection provided by the constitutional amendments and civil rights legislation, and the growing size of the Negro middle class. Whites would call it Negro progress from slavery to freedom toward equality.
>
> Negroes could point to the doctrine of white supremacy, its widespread acceptance, its persistence after emancipation, and its influence on the definition of the place of Negroes in American life. . . . They could see progress toward equality accompanied by bitter resistance. Perhaps most of all, they could feel the persistent, pervasive racism that kept them in inferior segregated schools, restricted them to ghettos, barred them from fair employment, provided double standards in courts of justice, inflicted bodily harm on their children, and blighted their lives with a sense of hopelessness and despair.[10]

The Gathering Storm

When the racial riots of the hot summer of 1967 erupted, a troubled and nervous nation asked: How can this happen to us? What is wrong? The panel of experts commissioned by the President to probe into the sources of the disorder alerted the public to the serious proportions of the crisis. In one sense it is impossible to "explain" a riot, as though on a stifling summer night residents of a ghetto or police in a riot squad act out of a cool and premeditated rational theory. But in another sense, there are many sufficient reasons, given the circumstances and the dark forces at work, why the explosions took place and are likely to continue. These forces can all be seen as various facets of our central problem: the terms of community according to which Negro and white are to live in America.

The outer, physical terms are set by the city. A major sociological factor in the American pattern of race relations has been the migration of the Negro from the rural South to the urban North and of the urban white man from the inner city to the suburbs.[11] The city residential pattern is that of the congested black ghetto tightly belted round by white suburbs. Within the ghetto, the pattern of life is one of increasing degradation and demoralization. A high rate of unemployment, alcoholism and drug addiction, sexual promiscuity and prostitution, thievery and violence, filth and squalor—these are the daily inevitable lot of millions. The Moynihan report pointed out that the close family unit has been "crumbling" in the face of the anonymity and crush of city living. "The family structure of lower class Negroes is highly unstable and in many urban centers is approaching complete break-down."[12] A shift from patriarchal to matriarchal authority, coupled with the mother's employment outside the home and the transient marital connections, all increase the instability of family relations. The Negro teen-ager identifies much more with his street gang than with his family. The alleys of the ghetto are haunted by *anomie* and alienation.

One facet of life in the city ghetto is especially ominous: the almost complete lack of personal contact between Negro and white. In the pattern of paternalistic relations in the small town or New South suburb, there was and is at least continual personal encounter at gas station and supermarket and kitchen which, despite the sinister bars of distance drawn by prejudice, keeps a kind of casual community of goodwill. In the ghetto these threads of communication are now completely cut. In the Watts section of Los Angeles, in Detroit, in Harlem, in South Chicago, it is a black world. The only encounter the Negro has with the white man's world is the hostile invasion of the white rent collector, or the police, or in the daily fare of the TV screen,[13] with its parade of promises of a white bourgeois chromium heaven, where white persons, redeemed from all bad breath and body odor, revel in the bliss of the barbecue by the swimming pool. The tantalizing promises of such a heaven, dangled in front of millions in the heated hells of the ghetto, heighten the tension between the promised expectation and the fact. For the white man's affluence, offered by TV on such quick and easy terms, is really out of the black man's reach, and becomes only a further provocation for him to grab for it. It is noteworthy that the chief object of looters in the summer riots are the color TV sets: they are the prizes that the poor both resent and covet. When one attempts to assess the causes of the riots, the TV set, celebrating as it does constantly in the presence of the forlorn and outcast, the affluence, the materialism, the violence, the sensualism of the white man's world, is certainly a chief culprit. And behind the TV set is the white commercial Establishment.

As the Kerner Commission Report documents, there seems to be a kind of dark conspiracy of forces, inner and outer, at work in increasing the tension. The city crowds its Negro poor into the ghetto, and with its automated economy can find few jobs other than menial ones. It expends its educational resources for the schools in the white suburbs, rather than for the inner-city Negro children. Meanwhile, inflation, no respecter of persons or classes, steadily lowers the real buying power of the poor man. All the while his real lot is deteriorating, he lives within sight of a promised land, the America of justice and equality assured him in political rhetoric and the sensate heaven assured him in the mass media. The very heightened expectation of a true community, of a fair land of equality and gentle ways, where all share gladly the benefits of prosperity, makes the Negro's present misery the more cruel, since daily the American dream is both promised and denied him.

An assessment of the sources of the mounting disorder, such as the Kerner Report details, points to the inexorable conclusion that beneath the outer environmental factors of urban congestion, summer heat, and the fortunes of the job market is the insidious conspiracy of white pride, prejudice, and power. In the last analysis, human sin is the source of the trouble. "White racism is essentially responsible for the explosive mixture which has been accumulating in our cities since the end of World War II."[14] The racism at the root of the matter is not as much the blatant, ugly sort of the Ku Klux Klansman, or the white quick-credit loan shark, or a Bull Connor, cruel and plain as this open racism is. The face of evil is rather more benign. It is the more polite variety of middle-class respectability that applauds greater justice for the Negro, generally speaking, but will support restrictive covenants in the neighborhood, that automatically associates lawlessness and violence with Negro looters, not with police brutality. Or it may be the racism of Madison Avenue, so slick as to seem almost innocent, which at once flaunts the blessings of the white American consumer before the eyes of the poor Negro and prevents him from having them.

The Rise of Black Power

In the light of these conditions, the rise of the Black Power movement is not at all strange. A new generation of militant, impatient young Negroes, in rebellion against the older liberal organizations working in more staid ways for racial equality, resentful as much of the hypocrisies and cautions of the white moderate as of the blatant racism of the white backlash, skeptical of the validity of nonviolence as a strategy in achieving racial change, are demanding full equality now.[15]

Much of what the Black Power spokesmen advocate is only an escalation of the persisting demands of civil rights causes and crusades for half a century and more. In terms of ends, Black Power seeks for the Negro full justice, full equality, full freedom in the opportunities and benefits of American society. But as to the means to achieve these goals, Black Power proposes that the Negro should go it alone. Only by cultivating an intense separate racial loyalty can the Negro throw off the stigma of inferiority that he has absorbed into his soul from the white man's world. The only way he can receive the white man's respect, he feels, is through developing his own black self-respect, through pride in his own separate identity. He wants therefore to cultivate a totally black economy and culture. In the name of common justice, should not schools, stores, transportation and entertainment facilities, business and legal institutions for blacks be owned and run by blacks? If the white man is slow to grant the moral point and reluctant to concede his power over the system, the black man proposes to take it, by whatever means at hand. If conventional and constitutional nonviolent means do not avail, or are exploited by the white man in power as a way of turning the beggars back, then violent methods are not precluded.

What moral assessment is to be made of the Black Power movement by the criteria of Christian community?

On the positive side, it first should readily be acknowledged that a pride in one's distinctive identity—in blackness, or in whiteness—represents a genuine response to the equality and diversity of the original community of the order of creation. To say "Black is beautiful" is an authentic expression of the love of God the Creator and his created order.

Secondly, the insistence of Black Power advocates that some real parity of power is a necessary precondition of social intercourse is more true to the terms of Christian community than the unequal power relations of paternalism and segregation that prevailed in the old order. In his assessment of the Black Power movement, Martin Luther King, Jr., has noted realistically that "we know through painful experience that freedom is never voluntarily given by the oppressor; it must be demanded by the oppressed."[16] This moral point has been confirmed in political experience, by voter registration drives. The Negro bloc vote, as a form of consolidated Black Power, has gradually made its gains in earning for the Negro a larger voice in political decision—but more despite white suspicion and resistance than with white liberal support.

Further on the positive side, it should be noted that the ultimate goals of the Black Power crusade, despite some looseness of its own rhetoric and journalistic distortion by a white press, are akin to those of Christian community: an integrated society of full freedom and equality. If by "integration" is meant assimilation of the black man into the middle-class white man's culture and values, into a white mainstream, then the new Negro says, "No." But if the integration is read to mean a "coalition" of equals, and the terms of community be defined pluralistically, as neither white-dominated nor black-dominated, in short as human community, Black Power advocates would say, "Yes," though the proximate concern is with the redressing of the power imbalance by building black pride in separated form.[17]

On the other side of the moral ledger, however, as judged by a Christian and not a white norm of the terms of community, the Black Power movement becomes vulnerable at many points. Despite its disclaimers, it is betrayed into its own form of racism. It is understandable that the victim of centuries of white oppression should come to expect his oppressor to be cruel and hypocritical. But when this attitude hardens into a prejudice, into the stereotype that the white man can be nothing but a hypocrite, that his generosity is only condescension from entrenched power, that he cannot be trusted to seek genuine equality—this is as plain prejudice as the opposite white stereotype of the Negro as inherently lazy and promiscuous. The wide extent of the white man's support for the cause of civil rights, for many at the sacrifice of fortune and reputation, for a few at the sacrifice of their very life, gives the lie to that prejudice and shatters that stereotype.

Further, a note of cynicism is evident in the understanding of the basis of political relationships. "One of the 'myths' of the liberal," says Carmichael, "proceeds from the premise that political coalitions can be sustained on a moral, friendly, or sentimental basis, or on appeals to conscience. We view this as a myth because we believe that political relations are based on self-interest: benefits to be gained and losses to be avoided. For the most part, man's politics is determined by his evaluation of material good and evil. Politics results from a conflict of interests, not of consciences."[18]

Speaking in Christian theological terms, one may say that such a view of human affairs is faulted at two points. For one, it lacks the Christian sense of sin, the awareness that racial prejudice is not a function of color but of humanity, that hence contrition for racial prejudice on both sides of the color line is a precondition for reconciled community. For another, its Hobbesian realism betrays Black Power into a cynicism that does not admit the workings of grace and forgiveness in men's racial relations. Since goodwill, altruism, and conscience are ruled out of politics by definition, the terms of community become those of "coalition," no better than a social contract or negative community, the armistice of competing groups who never transcend their self-interest. This is a great moral distance away from integration, where by the grace of God men are both compelled by outer law *and* impelled by a redeemed conscience within to live in glad and free brotherhood.

Christian Response to the Crisis

In the light of the mounting crisis, the polarization of power, and the threats of a civil war, what finally can be offered as guidelines for Christian racial action, responsible to the mandates of Christian community? Though the destruction and slaughter of summer riots have jolted the American citizen out of his blithe confidence that progress is gradual and easy, he may be stayed from despair by his trust that there is always the divine reprieve of grace, the opening for love's movement, even in the most closed-in extremity.

The goal is clear enough: a racially integrated society. Measured by the terms of Christian community, an integrated society would be marked by this syndrome of qualities: (1) a *pluralism* where the racial and ethnic variations would neither be obscured nor neglected, nor exalted into criteria of worth or rank, (2) a *freedom from* any arbitrary limitation put upon its members by reason of race, nationality, or religion, and thus a freedom *for* full participation in the economic, political and cultural life of the nation, and (3) a *justice* resting upon a parity of power of one group with another. Where these terms of community are accepted voluntarily, are observed in outer practice, and where a society through law guards itself against their abuse and violation—there, one may say, the will of God for human community is done on earth. Such a society is "open." Its relations are transmuted from interracial to interpersonal, for the racial factor in the network of exchange becomes quite secondary to nonracial factors in human attachments and detachments.

The goal is sufficiently clear. But what of strategy and means? In midsummer of 1967, in the wake of the tragic riots in dozens of American cities, the President of the United States simultaneously commissioned a distinguished panel of American citizens to study and report to the nation on the civil disorder and called for a National Day of Prayer for Peace and Reconciliation. Skeptics commented that "a prayer and a panel" would not redeem the times. Yet this presidential action can be taken as symbol of the double strategy required by responsible love, in obedience to the demands of Christian community. Both an inner change of heart and the massive outer change of institutions and laws are needful. Either without the other is naïve and irresponsible to the dynamics of the situation and of social change. The evangelist calls for a change of spirit. "Give your heart to Christ tonight, and all these social problems will be solved." But this is no solution at all, for it ignores the social matrix of the heart, and new social policy decisions that a changed heart brings. There may be an opposite naïveté, however, in the sophistication of the social engineer, who hopes that the appropriation of federal millions will buy racial peace and a just society. This strategy in itself may not suffice to alter the internal springs of hatred and white racism that the Kerner Report found to be at the heart of the problem. Thus, both a change of inner heart *and* a change of outer structures are imperative and inextricable.

The distinctive cast and style of love's inner work fitting to the needs of the racial crisis is the will to treat the neighbor as equal, in all circumstances, despite and within the inequalities and barriers drawn by a segregated and racist society. In the white man, this means a contrite heart before God, acknowledging his own secret sin in his confusing an integrated society with the white establishment, concern with condescension, and liberality with the self-parade of virtue. He will accept the rebuke and rejection of a Black Power advocate, yet keep community with him. Love's task is a patient, firm, unyielding will to forgiveness and reconciliation among equals who stand on the same parity of power. It means a will to cherish the other as a person primarily, and only secondarily as a case of color, and thus to weave the sustaining fabric of interpersonal community underneath the interracial relations. These same qualities would mark the presence of Christian love in the Negro response to the racial crisis. Insofar as he is a follower of Christ, he could well learn the lesson enacted in the life of Martin Luther King, Jr., that nonviolence is the morally preferable way to realize the integrated community. Violence evokes retaliatory violence. It polarizes further the alienated segments of community. Nonviolence, while no less resolute and militant for justice, outwits the wisdom of this world by loving the opposing neighbor into community.

Love's outer and public work is the drastic alteration of the outer conditioning circumstances of life for the Negro through massive environmental change: urban renewal, open-housing laws, desegregation and equalization of educational opportunity, integration of the police force, racial impartiality in the administration of law, job opportunity programs in the private and public sector—all the familiar proposals that have been advanced, and only on a small scale implemented. They all are concrete expressions of the social justice required by the terms of Christian community.

NOTES

1. The most significant of these is the National Advisory Commission on Civil Disorders, appointed by President Lyndon B. Johnson in 1967. Reference to the Commission's Report (Bantam Books, 1968) hereinafter will be made as the Kerner Report. The most extensive earlier study of race relations in America, Gunnar Myrdal's *An American Dilemma* (Harper & Brothers, 1944), has been considerably outdated as to the rate and intensity of social change but may be taken as still valid in its explanation of the inner factors constituting the dilemma.

2. See Chapters I and II above. Out of the considerable literature that sets American race relations within a Christian theological framework, the following are most relevant: Kyle Haselden, *The Racial Problem in Christian Perspective* (Harper & Brothers, 1959); George Kelsey, *Racism and the Christian Understanding of Man* (Charles Scribner's Sons, 1965). See also Waldo Beach: "A Theological Analysis of Race Relations," in Paul Ramsey (ed.), *Faith and Ethics: The Theology of H. Richard Niebuhr.*

3. John Hope Franklin, *From Slavery to Freedom* (Alfred A. Knopf, Inc., 1947); C. Vann Woodward, *The Strange Career of Jim Crow* (rev. ed., Oxford University Press, Inc., 1957) are standard. Chapter 5, "Rejection and Protest: An Historical Sketch," of the Kerner Report summarizes well the more recent developments.

4. Cf. *Brown* vs. *Board of Education.* Opinion of the United States Supreme Court, May 17, 1954.

5. A close study of the phenomenon of prejudice which confirms in many ways a Christian reading of the matter is Gordon Allport's *The Nature of Prejudice* (abridged, Doubleday & Company, Inc., 1958).

6. Martin Luther King, Jr.'s thought was articulated in the sequence of these books: *Stride Toward Freedom* (Harper & Brothers, 1958); *Strength to Love* (Harper & Row, Publishers, Inc., 1963); *Why We Can't Wait* (The New American Library, Inc., 1964); *Where Do We Go from Here: Chaos or Community?* (Harper & Row, Publishers, Inc., 1967); and *The Trumpet of Conscience* (Harper & Row, Publishers, Inc., 1968), published after his assassination.

7. Chapter VI of *Stride Toward Freedom* is an autobiographical account of these influences.

8. King, *Strength to Love,* Ch. V.

9. See Andrew Kopkind, "Soul Power," a review of King's *Where Do We Go from Here?* in the *New York Review of Books,* Aug. 24, 1967, for a sharp indictment of King's whole strategy.

10. The Kerner Report, p. 235.

11. *Ibid.,* Ch. 6, "The Formation of the Racial Ghettos." Since 1940, 3.7 million Southern Negroes have migrated North. Within a decade, it is prophesied that a dozen major cities will join Washington, D.C., and Newark in having Negro majorities.

12. Daniel Moynihan, *The Negro Family* (U.S. Department of Labor, Office of Policy Planning and Research, 1965), Ch. II.

13. The TV set is to be found even in the shabbiest slum. According to census figures, in June, 1967, 87.7 percent of non-white households had television sets (Kerner Report, p. 376).

14. Kerner Report, p. 203.

15. The so-called Black Power movement does not have as coherent and articulated a rationale behind its slogan as did, for example, the Southern Christian Leadership Conference in Martin Luther King, Jr. Possibly the best source for the ideology of the movement is Stokely Carmichael and Charles V. Hamilton: *Black Power: The Politics of Liberation in America* (Vintage Book, Random House, Inc., 1967). Martin Luther King, Jr., *Where Do We Go from Here: Chaos or Community?* (Ch. II) makes a careful moral assessment of the movement from a Christian point of view as do Charles Fager, *White Reflections on Black Power* (Wm. B. Eerdmans Publishing Company, 1967); Joseph C. Hough, Jr., *Black Power and White Protestants* (Oxford University Press, Inc., 1968); and Nathan Wright, Jr., *Black Power and Urban Unrest* (Hawthorn Books, Inc., 1967). The most accurate journalistic treatments of current trends are to be found in *Newsweek.* William Brink and Louis Harris, *Black and White: A Study of U.S. Racial Attitudes Today* (Simon and Schuster, Inc., 1967), puts the *Newsweek* survey findings into a single volume.

16. From "Letter from Birmingham City Jail," reprinted in King, *Why We Can't Wait,* p. 80.

17. "Ultimately, the gains of our struggle will be meaningful only when consolidated by viable coalitions between blacks and whites who accept each other as co-equal partners and who identify their goals as politically and economically similar." (Carmichael and Hamilton, *op. cit.,* p. 84).

18. Carmichael and Hamilton, *op. cit.,* p. 75.

IX

Christian Community and the American University

As now we turn to examine and assess the academic community in America by the norms of Christian community, we will be engaging in a review of many matters discussed earlier. For though the university or college has its distinctive qualities, it also obviously mirrors the values of its culture in its educational goals and practices. It may talk of leading its culture by training an intelligent elite, and in a measure it does. It may stand away as critic of its society, to expose its tawdry values and Philistine affections, and in a measure it does. But also the university caters closely to the values of its culture. Behind the talk and the pose, one can detect readily on campus the same haunting powers of *anomie* and alienation and the same tribal deities of scientism, materialism, and sensualism that bewitch American culture at large. The university follows as much as it leads American society.

How can one speak of *the* American university in the face of the manifold variety of schools listed in any education directory? Though all may bear the name university, they share only a family name. What common *ethos* is shared by the huge California university system and the small New England college? A hundred years ago, such an analysis as this might take the college as the normative type and ask: What makes the college a Christian community? But in the twentieth century, the small college has grown into the large university and become quite a different kind of place. The more it becomes a factory or a city of itself, the more nostalgically it cultivates the presiding symbols of home, to elicit alumni support and foster loyalty to Alma Mater, who draws her children back for Homecoming in the fall. The presiding symbol is the old green campus of the small college. In reality, the large university sets the pattern and style for all schools, large or small. The same styles of intellectual dress prevail for all. The college aspires to do the same thing on a smaller scale that the university is doing en masse. Although indeed there are considerable differences in size and quality and spirit between the church-related and state-supported schools, some generalizations may hold good for them all.

In common American imagery there is an aura of sanctity hovering over the university campus. It is a blessed place. There seems to be an almost unlimited trust of Americans in the benefits of higher education, as witnessed by the billions poured from federal and private funds into the vast building programs of the universities and the bustle with which every small city sets up its community college. No one without a college education can really presume to belong or to have what it takes. The subtle processes of ranking and status in the business and political world may be made more on the basis of the quality of a man's college than of his home or church. It may not be too much to say that the campus has surpassed the home and the church, in the American's value scale, as the institution that is trusted as the savior of society, the paradigm of perfect community, where youth are all trained to intelligent maturity and gracious living.

Yet on occasion this aura of sanctity is jarred, if not shattered, by an explosion. The riots at Berkeley and Columbia and many other schools troubled the American dream about the idyllic university with a sudden nightmare. The Easter bacchanalias on Florida beaches are somewhat less genteel than the sober proprieties of June baccalaureates. The widespread use of narcotics and hallucinogenic drugs does not seem to give sign of intelligent maturity. A glimpse behind the ivy-covered walls into a dormitory bull session reveals something less than an eager passion for learning or responsible and considerate student self-government.

While universities expand apace and enrollments soar, there is widespread soul-searching among educators about the inner failure of nerve that besets the university culture. The most bothersome questions are the issues of this book: What are the terms of authentic community that make a university *one?* Is its trouble a case of lost or mistaken identity? What factors conspire to tear the fabric of community and what forces are at hand to restore it? Such questions lead beyond purely technical considerations and matters of educational psychology or philosophy into moral and, in the last analysis, theological issues.[1]

The Disintegration of the American University

Critics and diagnosticians of higher education in America may display something of the same nostalgia for the Golden Days of the past as the urban sociologist may have for the simple beauties of country life, or church historians for the "pristine purity" of the early church. They forget that the Golden Days were never really that golden. Any memories of a simple unity of the medieval European university, or of an eighteenth-century Harvard Yard where all was peaceful intellectual unanimity, obscures, in the gentle haze of hindsight, the tensions and controversies that no doubt erupted. The nominalist-realist controversy of the Schoolmen and the warfare of science and theology were hardly placid. Heads rolled in the battles over truth. But by contrast to the contemporary university, there *was* a high degree of intellectual unity in a commonly shared world view. To go back only a century or so in American higher education, if one examines the curriculum of the liberal arts college in New England, one finds a close unity of subjects in classics, natural sciences, English, etc., with a senior capstone course in moral philosophy, taught by the president of the college, a churchman and theologian. The currency of intellectual exchange was that of Protestant Christianity. The chapel was at the architectural and emotional center of the campus, where the spiritual and moral purposes of higher learning were celebrated in common worship. No doubt the faculty meetings, though opened with prayer, were ridden with political infighting. No doubt there were student protests, if not riots.[2] No doubt the intellectual waters were not always calm. But the strong sense of identity in a Christian world view gave the original college a high degree of integrity of mind.[3]

The complex story of the shift from this unified college of a century ago to the multiversity of today is a familiar one.[4] The first form of disintegration is an *intellectual* one. The gradual change from the authority of theology to the authority of science, the proliferation of the curriculum in the "free elective" system, the multiplication of professions for which the university trained its students, the religious and ethnic pluralism in the American college population, the sheer bulk of numbers of students—all have had their disintegrative effect. The end result has been "the multiversity," with a curriculum splintered into fragments, where the relation of courses to each other is one only of "simultaneity and juxtaposition," as William Temple once noted, and where faculty find no common meeting ground of shared intellectual premises but can talk only with those in their own field. One of its sharpest critics, Robert Hutchins, defined the university as a group of buildings and schools that share a common heating plant.

This fragmentation of a structured body of truth into scattered truths that bear no organic relation to one another: here is the anarchy, the *anomie* of the modern American university, copied in turn by the small college.

Hutchins described *anomie* on campus thus: "The crucial error is that of holding that nothing is more important than anything else, that there can be no order of goods, and no order in the intellectual realm, that there is nothing central, nothing peripheral, nothing primary, nothing secondary, nothing basic, and nothing superficial. The course of study goes to pieces because there is nothing to hold it together."[5] The purported community of scholars united in a common search for truth is splintered into departments and schools, each in political and ideological rivalry with all others, each suspicious of the intellectual credentials of any discipline but its own. In the estimate of any one professor, the titles of Ph.D. dissertations in any other field than his specialty seem like the height of triviality. "Why do they waste their time studying things like that?"

So *anomie,* pride, and myopic vision pervert the purposes of the university. And the psychological consequences are the moods of alienation and apathy in the motivations of both faculty and student. The image may be that of the teacher-scholar engrossed in disinterested research or leading the eager student by the hand into the spacious Temple of Wisdom. The reality is somewhat different. Professionalism of the system perverts research into the frantic publish-or-perish grind. The teacher is compelled by the system to stretch each student onto the Procrustean bed of the course requirements. The student, on his part, is alienated from the pursuit of truth into a melancholy apathy, from which he will be prodded only by the requirements of the system to study for grades, to pass courses, to do enough to get through. The disciplines intended to lead the student to responsible maturity in truth-seeking to a considerable degree may thwart that end. The idolatry of grades may require the sacrifice of honor, where, to stay in the game, the student may be forced by the system to cheat on exams. So the congenial community of scholars is turned into the competitive society of pedants and operators, in endless anxious skirmishes and political battles with each other.

To be sure, this dire picture is overdrawn for emphasis, and should quickly be corrected by the acknowledgment that there is much eager learning and exciting teaching going on, that the various programs for integration are healthy moves toward wholeness of mind. But in the broad overview, the vital experiments and the integrative efforts go against the main drift of things.

The second form of disintegration of the university is *social,* in the living relationships of its members. Unlike the European university, which bears responsibility for academic relations only, from the start the American university has been a resident community where some outer terms of community relations have to be set. The dominant pattern set by the older college was the authoritarian paternalistic model of the home, where the college, acting *in loco parentis,* prescribed carefully the rules of behavior for the children in its care. Close community controls by deans and a bevy of housemothers, it was hoped, would protect virginity and cultivate the Christian proprieties.[6] Chapel was the sign of the presence of a divine chaperon and monitor. The limited size of the student body was itself a social control and gave each student a sense of accountability, for he was known and watched by his peers, if God should not for the moment be looking.

Quite the opposite situation prevails in the contemporary university. Partly this is the consequence of sheer numbers. In a university of 30,000 students the individual is frightened and lost. There is an inverse ratio between density of mass and sense of personal identity. Known intimately by no one, though he hails many acquaintances on his rounds, the individual feels anonymous. He rushes from circle to circle, hunting for his "real self," but his college career is generally a low-pitched "identity crisis." The incidents of student suicides and the number of psychiatric counseling cases, while of no greater ratio than in society at large, are still shattering to any blissful image of "bright college years."

Community depends on vital, trusted communications. When a campus becomes too large, the communication among its segments breaks down from what Kenneth Boulding has called the Brontosaurus principle. It becomes too big to cope with itself.[7]

The moral disintegration of the campus is as much due to *anomie* within as to mass of numbers without. This form of the crisis in community derives from the absence of any accepted terms of political authority, any common norms of diverse rights and obligations for the various segments, faculty, trustees, administration, and students. "There is no King in Israel." The paternalistic pattern of authority has been gradually eroded. A nervous administration may be tolerant and permissive, partly to foster student responsibility, but more out of considerable moral uncertainty as to what *are* indeed proper modes of campus behavior. The bewildered faculty avoid dealing with the problem of student behavior and pass by on the other side. It is none of their business.

On their part, students are in revolt against paternalism, against conventional standards, against the phony strictures of their parents or any authoritarian figure, in a widespread seething rebellion. But their rebellion gives mark of the same *anomie* which is one ingredient in the administration's permissiveness. Students are rebels, but often with no cause beyond protest itself.[8] They want a larger voice in setting the terms of social relationships, but are not at all sure what the obligations are that make the exercise of larger rights viable. The surly vociferous minority, where not engaged in prolonged thumb-sucking and navel-gazing, do battle with the administration or the dean's office, the Enemy by definition, for setting stupid parietal hours and for its breach of contract in failing to make life more pleasant for the tuition-paying customers.

The student attitude toward morality reveals a curious ambivalence: a strict conformity to prevailing fashions of the in-group in dress, mores, morals, and even theological beliefs, and on the other side a kind of "live and let live" tolerance of variant behavior, on matters of sex ethics or smoking pot, or treatment of campus property, reflecting a complete individualism. The college student is morally certain of one thing only: he is not his brother's keeper. Anything goes as long as nobody gets hurt. It may be that *anomie* accounts for both the intolerance and the tolerance; by strict conformity, by going along closely with the boys, one may cover over his inner moral confusion, while the tolerance expresses more of an uncertainty of conviction than a respect for conscientious differences.

This picture of the university betrays the slovenly use of the big brush. It is indeed a harsh cartoon that surely should be qualified at many points. Matters are really not all that anomic; the reality is an encouraging and discouraging mixture. In the vast lonely sea of the state campus, here and there students find islands of authentic community. In many progressive colleges, where students *are* given a genuine voice in determining their affairs, they exercise their freedom responsibly. In the very ferment and revolt, there is search for new norms, and new terms of identity, new wine that breaks the old wineskins.

Toward the Recovery of Christian Community

To a university president seeking a road out of chaos to coherence or to a floundering student asking for one good reason why he should stay with it, the suggestion that there is relevance in the Christian tradition for the problems of *anomie* and alienation may seem like a quaint archaism. "Back to God" or "Come to Christ" would appear slogans of escape rather than serious confrontations with the problems here diagnosed. There is wisdom in the academic suspicion of an instant cure sometimes proffered in the formulas of the Christian faith. One must be careful in distinguishing the false claims from the true claims to relevance of Christianity to the university.

It would be false to attempt to impose on its mind some one scheme of Christian doctrine, for this violates the basic commitment of the university to the free and unproscribed search for truth. Theology, in the sense of a structured system of truths, is no longer—if ever she were—the queen of the sciences, who now, however tacky she may appear, should be restored to her throne. To attempt to recover out of the Babel of tongues of the campus classroom a common universe of discourse in the classic terms of Christian theology, by showing how biology, sociology, psychology, history, literature, economics, and whatever can somehow be fitted within the Apostles' Creed or the Thirty-Nine Articles or the Westminster Confession, would be artificial and distorted. Even if possible, it would be an instance of gross theological imperialism.

There are some attempts at keeping the integral university centered in mind around Christian doctrine, most notably in Roman Catholic schools.[9] The scholastic system of truth is here the integrating core. In practice, however, as many Catholic educators concede, the integration is fragile at best: the Thomistic scheme is laid alongside the newer sciences without genuine inner connection achieved.[10] Another attempt to hold higher education under the control of Christian belief is in the "Bible colleges" of the evangelical and fundamentalist denominations. But these schools generally violate the essential ground rules of a university, proscribing the lines of research and teaching by an incredible Biblical literalism, and attempting to rest too much on too narrow a base.[11] To require the teacher of psychology or sociology to conform his subject matter to a narrow Biblicism is to violate the integrity of his discipline and to subject universality of truth to parochial dogma.

We would maintain that such attempts at reintegration around any prescribed body of Christian truths, however ardent and pious, do not provide viable answers to the university question. Their likely impact on an intelligent faculty member or student is to encourage duplicity or legitimate rebellion. In this sense we would concur with the statement of the Harvard Report on General Education, made some years ago, that "religion is not now for most colleges a practicable source of intellectual unity."[12]

But there is quite another way to approach the problem of intellectual chaos. It has to do with the loves of the heart rather than the sight of the mind, with motivation and stance of spirit in teaching and research and study, rather than with true or false conclusions. In the life of its mind, the members of a university community may be made one out of many, integrated out of chaos, by a shared allegiance in the love of God. The intellectual form of the love of God does not mean subscription to any credal statement about the nature of God or his action in history. It means rather a reverence in the face of mystery, a trustful curiosity, a restless, searching, doubting, affirming spirit of wonder, sustained by the tacit confidence that there is an order of truth beyond and within the manifold puzzle of the present disorder. As put by H. Richard Niebuhr: "Love to God is conviction that there is faithfulness at the heart of things—unity, reason, form and meaning in the plurality of being."[13] This is the common faith that makes an assembly of scholars into a community, beneath their plural traditional religious persuasions and the strife of schools and systems that constitute the dynamics of the university's daily life. The scholar coming out of the

Roman Catholic tradition might phrase this conviction by affirming that the order of being and the order of value are one. A Protestant way of putting it would be to say that men are justified, as an intellectual community, by the trust of their hearts that there is meaning in the mystery, and that their scholarly work is a response to grace. Even the agnostic, the radical questioner, shares in this community of faith, at least in the sense that he must presume an order of truth for his very questioning of it to be intelligible.

A most important implication of this understanding of the responsible love of God in the life of the mind is for epistemology, or the perennial problem of knowledge. One basic force that appears to divide the mind of the campus is the so-called split between faith and reason, producing the division between the faithful and the faithless. "Faith" is often taken to mean blind assent to a body of dogma, the stance of the religious man. "Reason" is taken to mean everything that goes under the heading of "scientific method," a critical, cautious, experiential approach to data, where everything must be confirmed by experiment and testing. By such a division in method, of course, the theologian cannot really talk with the scientist on campus, since they do not agree about the basic rules of the hunt.

As we have already been at pains to explain,[14] this stark dualism between faith and reason is false. In every major discipline of study, both faith *and* reason operate together. In the sciences, faith operates as primal assumption or hypothesis on which critical investigation proceeds. All investigation and analysis, microscopic or macroscopic, of enzymes or galaxies, is faithful thinking, sustained by a trust that there is an intelligible order in the phenomena studied. Likewise, good theological thinking is not blindly credulous but self-critical, scrupulous in its treatment of evidence and the laws of thought, alert always to check its tenets against experience. So, as much in theological as in scientific reflection, there is faithful reasoning and critical faith. For theologian as much as for scientist or philosopher, doubt is not the foe but the friend of understanding. For doubt keeps faith from credulity, as trust keeps reason from skepticism. The explicit appreciation of this basic ground rule for the community of learning would do much to overbridge the gulf between the sciences and the humanities, and provide an epistemological reconciliation. In this spirit, all members of the university would share in that openness and tentativity which is the wisdom of "scientific method." All parties to the dialogue might concur with the judgment of a seventeenth-century divine that "man hath but a shallow sound and a short reach and deals only with probabilities and likelihoods." Yet a person of intellectual contrition before God is not the radical skeptic or nihilist. He is as trustful that there is ultimate meaning in the mystery as he is distrustful and provisional in his claim for the little part he grasps.

The relevance of theology in recovering community of mind in the university is not to be found, then, by attempting to restore her as queen of the sciences, but by finding her as servant.[15] In this role, theology is not so much a separate subject in the curriculum—though it is legitimately that—as it is a certain dimension of all subjects. Theology should bother each classroom, from mechanical engineering to metaphysical poetry, with the great questions of the meaning of human existence. It should haunt each finite truth with the intimations of infinity. It should point each fact, each person, each event beyond itself to a universal community. Out of this love of God, the members of the scholarly community can serve each other by mutual limitation in a system of checks and balances in a democracy of learning. The scientist, observing rigor and exactitude, may correct the religion teacher's fuzziness, while the teacher of religion may serve the scientist by raising the questions about ends for means, or the moral uses of the power of technology, questions that technology is powerless to answer of itself. So some close sense of interdependence may restore community among students of independent disciplines.

Social Reconciliation

We have traced earlier the social disintegration and *anomie* of the university, the breakdown of the traditional structures of paternalistic authority, and the revolt of students. What relevance does Christian love have to this perplexing aspect of the university's social life? Again, as with the problem of its disintegration of mind, we set aside the quick remedies of Religious Emphasis Week or the simple prescriptions of the evangelist. But there is an indirect relevance of the great commandment that might be traced out, which provides guidelines for social reintegration.

The university community is not of course a community of only intellectual transaction; it is a community of total persons. Like all communities, it exists in precarious equilibrium between the centrifugal and centripetal thrusts, between the cohesive pull of loyalty and obligation, and the scattering drive for rights and privileges. When the centrifugal drive for rights has no countervailing impulse of obligations, the community flies apart into anarchy. The dominant drive on the American campus is the centrifugal one, the pursuit of rights. Whereas the architectural center of the nineteenth-century campus was the chapel, symbolizing and honoring integrative obligations, the center of the twentieth-century campus is the new Student Union building, complete with bowling alleys and TV lounges—dedicated to the cultivation of student privileges and comforts. Many a student comes to the university on the assumption that college education is primarily a privilege and that life there should be so organized as to provide him a maximum of happiness. The chief question he asks is: Are they nice to me? Do they make me happy?

A Christian counterattack for the recovery of community must be more inward than the devices of the dean's office in setting the outer limits of decent behavior, necessary as these are. No legalism really gets at the problem of social responsibility. The return to community lies by way of the recovery of an inner morale derived from responsible love. What can give a Christian moral tone to the university is the shared allegiance of all its members to the well-being of the others, the common persuasion that each is responsible to God for his neighbor in concern and respect. Responsibility in love provides the cohesive force that reconciles the community from its brokenness and sustains it in trust underneath the inevitable collisions of the interests of its parts and the diffusions of its pursuit of rights.

The university professor, for his part, might discover his Christian vocation or identity in cultivating the personal equation within the cracks of the impersonal system. "He took a personal interest in me." This is one of the tributes that students pay to the memorable teacher. This "personal interest" does not mean the chumminess of the "operator," who seeks first a high rating in the student evaluation poll. The "personal interest" may be exacting and rigorous in its intellectual demands, for Christian love is accountable to God for the neighbor. The authentic teacher's love is sensitive to the whimsies and talents and shortcomings of his student, but not sentimental or soft. The vocation of the Christian teacher, by the terms of the great commandment, is to be the mediator of a sacred order of truth to a sacred order of persons. "Thou shalt love the Lord thy God." This means, in research and writing, in laboratory and classroom, a careful regard for the order of truth, in all its elusive and compelling mystery. "Thou shalt love thy neighbor as thyself." This means the teacher is befriending his student as a sacred "Thou," infinitely precious.

We speak here, to be sure, in a highly normative vein. How can a teacher have a personal regard for that one student about to knock on his office door when the student is one of sixty in a class and when the teacher's life is cluttered with committees, chores, articles overdue, the next class, etc., etc.? A nineteenth-century definition of the ideal college was "Mark Hopkins on one end of a log and a student on the other," but a twentieth-century Mark Hopkins may be so busy at logrolling in the political jungle of the university that he never can sit on it and talk with a student. The system seems the implacable enemy of community, and personal love an impossible demand. Yet there are niches and crannies in the system where men do find reconciliation, partial though it be, to the order of truth and to each other.

The administration, for its part, is put under obligation by the great commandment to seek to make the system it administers instrumental to the good of persons within it. This means that the dean, as the faculty member, would see the "mature manhood" of the student as the end for which all the regulations should be directed, and for whom, if need be, they should be abrogated. In the face of a surging student protest and clamor for a larger voice, or for "participatory democracy," the president is by the terms of responsible love required to listen in patience, to sift as best he can the legitimate from the illegitimate claims, to risk extensions of freedoms on the capital of proven student responsibilities, and at the same time to explain his obligations to constituents of the university community—parents, trustees, alumni—other than the students, and to point out that students' demands may not coincide exactly with the students' real needs. This may not avail to satisfy the students, but it will be a stance of responsible love, and it may keep open the lines of trusted communication throughout a controversy.

The student, for his part, may recover his identity in Christian vocation also under the terms of responsible love for God and neighbor. This does not mean a Pharisaic parade of piety or necessarily a public declaration for Christ. It means, in the secret places, a shift of motivation in study from the egocentric to the theocentric. It means that the student sees the university as the place where he may equip himself to fulfill the law of love in service to the larger community.

"Knowledge is in order to goodness." This Calvinistic phrase is pertinent to the issue of the motivation for study. In one sense, surely, the pursuit of truth in the university is disinterested, morally neutral. It is prostituted when turned to any partisan purpose of church or state. But in another sense, technical knowledge *cannot* be morally neutral, for it is always held as a tool in the hand of a living person who has loyalties and antipathies, loves and hates, who will use his knowledge to advance his espoused causes, be they malevolent or benevolent. Whether the educated person tears or strengthens the fabric of community depends not on the extent of his information but on the sensitivity of his conscience and the bent of his will. His will may be bent inward to himself. He may treat his college education as a rehearsal for the comforts and privileges of status in the affluence of suburbia. With such a *voluntas* he will regard his citizenship in the college community as something of a contract whereby his parents pay the college to allow him the pursuit of his happiness. Or, his will may be bent outward to the needs of neighbor, by *agape*. He may treat his college as a covenant community of which he is a junior member, so to speak, obliged by the terms of the covenant to study to become not a parasite or ornament, but a servant of society. For whatever secular profession he trains, this is his Christian vocation whereby he fulfills his citizenship in the Kingdom of God.

Now, given the mixture of sin and grace abounding in every empirical university, it is plain that any given student group in any given dormitory could not be sorted into two bins: the pagans of inturned wills, the saints of outer-turned wills. What is here drawn is more of a psychological than a sociological division. Any single student is at heart a tussle of contrary wills. But one may yet realistically discern, in the moral mixture, preponderant tendencies of will and crucial orientations of purpose. Insofar as the will to learn to serve is predominant, to that degree one may declare the presence of Christian community in that person and on that campus.

What has just been said is cast in normative and prescriptive terms. This is not entirely idle moralizing, however, for there is much empirical evidence on campus for a strong student response to the needs of community. Through participation in the civil rights movement, or a tutoring program in the Negro ghettos, or a summer work camp project, or the Peace Corps, a student who may have been turned in on himself may be flung out in engagement with desperate human need and led to find himself by losing himself in service to neighbor. His impatience with the staid and cloistered niceties of his courses back on campus, and his demand for the relevance of the academic to the human situation is a sign of grace, of *agape* overcoming *anomie,* for it marks his personal search for identification with Christian community.[16]

NOTES

1. The literature of self-examination of higher education is vast. A useful and full bibliography, especially of religious and ethical issues, is to be found in Manning Patillo and Donald MacKenzie, *Church-sponsored Higher Education in the United States* (American Council on Education, 1966), pp. 279–295. The older studies of Moberly, Nash, and Coleman are useful background. Denis Baly, *Academic Illusion* (The Seabury Press, Inc., 1961), and the current writings of Paul Goodman are sharp indictments of American higher education, one from a Christian, the other from a humanistic perspective. Daniel Bell, *The Reforming of General Education* (Columbia University Press, 1966), and David Riesman, *Constraint and Variety in American Education* (Doubleday & Company, Inc., 1958), are important contributions. The most important and full recent study is Christopher Jencks and David Riesman, *The Academic Revolution* (Doubleday & Company, Inc., 1968).

2. At Harvard's first commencement, in 1642, complaint was made against two young men, "of good quality, lately come out of England, for foul misbehavior, in swearing and ribaldry speeches, etc." The Board gave the president authority to flog the students, which was done as soon as the exercises were over. (Howard Lowry, *The Mind's Adventure: Religion and Higher Education* [The Westminster Press, 1950], p. 41.)

3. To cite another instance, this advertisement for King's College (later Columbia University) appeared in the *New York Gazette* for June 3, 1754: "The chief thing that is aimed at in this college is to teach and engage the children to know God in Jesus Christ, and to love and serve him, in all sobriety, godliness, and righteousness of life, with a perfect heart and a willing mind" (Lowry, *op. cit.,* p. 43). One wonders what the reaction would be of the "children" who occupied the buildings on Morningside Heights in May of 1968 to such a statement of Columbia's educational purpose.

4. The American experience has followed closely Moberly's account of the four stages of development of the European university: (1) Christian-Hellenic, (2) liberal, (3) technological and democratic, (4) chaotic. Walter Moberly, *The Crisis in the University* (London: SCM Press, Ltd., 1949).

5. Robert Hutchins, *Education for Freedom* (Louisiana State University Press, 1943), p. 26. The recent discussion sparked by *The Two Cultures and the Scientific Revolution* (London: Cambridge University Press, 1959) of C. P. Snow reflects the same discontent with the split mind of the university.

6. One sectarian college in the Midwest once advertised itself to prospective students and fearful, pious parents as located "seven miles from any known sin."

7. Kenneth Boulding, *The Organizational Revolution,* p. 63. The post-mortem analyses of the Berkeley and Columbia riots point to the lack of any regular channels of communication as a major factor in the explosion. Seymour Lipset and Sheldon Wolin, *The Berkeley Student Revolt* (Doubleday & Company, Inc., 1965).

8. Kenneth Keniston, *The Uncommitted: Alienated Youth in American Society* (Harcourt, Brace and World, Inc., 1965).

9. For representative materials, see "Declaration on Christian Education," in Walter M. Abbott, S.J. (ed.), *The Documents of Vatican II,* or John Courtney Murray, *We Hold These Truths* (Sheed & Ward, Inc., 1960), Ch. 5, "Creeds at War Intelligibly."

10. The noble experiment of Hutchins at the University of Chicago to integrate all knowledge around metaphysics came to grief among other reasons because the kind of metaphysical scheme proposed could not contain the vitalities of modern sciences.

11. See Larry C. King, "Bob Jones University: The Buckle on the Bible Belt," *Harper's Magazine* (June, 1966), for an example of the bizarre consequences of an attempt to conform all truths to the Bible.

12. Harvard Committee, *General Education in a Free Society* (Harvard University Press, 1945), p. 39.

13. H. Richard Niebuhr, *The Purpose of the Church and Its Ministry* (Harper & Brothers, 1956), p. 37. A further articulation of Niebuhr's position is to be found in "Theology in the University" in the volume *Radical Monotheism and Western Culture.*

14. See Chapter IV above, pp. 67–73.

15. H. Richard Niebuhr, *Radical Monotheism and Western Culture,* pp. 98 ff.

16. There is, of course, a mountain of literature reporting and analyzing "the student mind" in America, from *Playboy* and *Look* to elaborate studies of particular campus phenomena, such as Lipset and Wolin, *op. cit.* The journal containing the most lively discussions of the religious dimension of the university has been *The Christian Scholar,* published by the Commission on Higher Education of the National Council of Churches. Though *The Christian Scholar* suspended publication as of 1967, its interests are continued in a new journal, *Soundings: A Journal of Interdisciplinary Studies,* published under the sponsorship of the Society on Religion in Higher Education.

Index

Date Due

Demco 38-297